HOPE FOR
THIS
PRESENT
CRISIS

HOPE FOR
THIS
PRESENT
CRISIS

MICHAEL YOUSSEF

FRONT
LINE

Most Charisma House Book Group products are available at special quantity discounts for bulk purchase for sales promotions, premiums, fund-raising, and educational needs. For details, call us at (407) 333-0600 or visit our website at www.charismahouse.com.

Hope for This Present Crisis by Michael Youssef
Published by FrontLine
Charisma Media/Charisma House Book Group
600 Rinehart Road, Lake Mary, Florida 32746

Unless otherwise noted, all Scripture quotations are taken from the Holy Bible, New International Version®, niv®. Copyright © 1973, 1978, 1984, 2011 by Biblica, Inc.® Used by permission of Zondervan. All rights reserved worldwide. www.zondervan.com. The "niv" and "New International Version" are trademarks registered in the United States Patent and Trademark Office by Biblica, Inc.®

Scripture quotations marked kjv are from the King James Version of the Bible.

Visit the author's website at ltw.org,
www.thispresentcrisis.com.

Library of Congress Cataloging-in-Publication Data:
An application to register this book for cataloging has
been submitted to the Library of Congress.
International Standard Book Number:
978-1-62999-864-0
E-book ISBN: 978-1-62999-865-7

21 22 23 24 25 — 9 8 7 6 5 4 3 2 1
Printed in the United States of America

To all the faithful pastors, teachers,
and preachers who proclaim
the truth of the Word of God
without compromise

Once to every man and nation comes the moment to decide,
In the strife of Truth with Falsehood, for the good or evil side.

—THE PRESENT CRISIS,
JAMES RUSSELL LOWELL, 1845

CONTENTS

INTRODUCTION

OUR PRESENT CRISIS

I HAVE BEEN WRITING this book during a time of global crisis—or rather, multiple global crises. There was a crisis known as the coronavirus (COVID-19) pandemic, which triggered another global crisis, the worldwide economic shutdown. Amid these crises, civil unrest erupted across America, with protesters and rioters setting fires, looting shops, and tearing down statues and monuments from Seattle and Los Angeles to New York and Atlanta.

But none of these crises are the present crisis that I've written about in this book. There's an even greater crisis that confronts our civilization today, and this book is a warning of the destruction that is yet to come upon our land if we do not *act now* in obedience to God's Word.

Even though this book is not about the pandemic, the coronavirus crisis is a sobering reminder that our government, military might, economic power, and technological wizardry are all amazingly vulnerable to a submicroscopic organism. It is a virus so small it can only be seen with an electron microscope. Yet this invisible threat has shaken the foundations of human society and brought mighty corporations and governments to their knees.

But our God is sovereign and in control of world events. This virus did not take Him by surprise. God is not wringing His hands and saying, "What should I do?" He controls every breath we take. He controls every beat of our hearts. He is in control of our lives from birth to death. A crisis should not signal Christians to panic; it should ignite our faith and increase our obedience. We must not let our hearts be troubled.

I hope and pray that by the time you read these words, the pandemic will be history, the civil unrest will subside, the economy will stabilize, and your life will return to normal. But even when these tumultuous times have passed, we must never forget that an even more dangerous crisis still confronts us. Like the COVID-19 virus, this present crisis is spreading invisibly throughout our society. It affects every one of us, though most of us are completely unaware of it.

> **A crisis should not signal Christians to panic; it should ignite our faith and increase our obedience.**

Simply put, this present crisis is the decline of the influence of the Christian church. All across America and Europe, churches are emptying, and an entire generation is turning away from God. People today have many gods—money, pleasure, politics, the environment—but they no longer acknowledge the God of the Bible. The devaluing of the family and human life has led to countless abortions, fewer marriages, and more empty cradles. Social scientists who once warned of a population *explosion* now warn of a population *implosion*, as birth rates are declining disastrously in Western nations.[1]

The traditional values and social bonds that once held our society together are disintegrating, along with traditional Christian-based morality. Addiction, suicide, and crime are epidemic in Western society. The internet and social media, once thought to be bringing the world together, have unleashed humanity's most hateful, sinful urges, dividing people into warring tribes. This is our present crisis—not an external threat from terrorists or warlike nations or a viral pandemic, but a decline of faith, truth, and morality. It is hollowing out our society from within.

We in the West have assumed that our democratic institutions, culture, and way of life would go on forever. We expected our economy to always be strong, our military to remain invulnerable, and our traditions to endure. But empires and civilizations have collapsed again and again in the past. As former US Comptroller General David M. Walker warns, Western society today shows signs of imminent collapse.

> Many of us think that a superpowerful, prosperous nation like America will be a permanent fixture dominating the world scene. We are too big to fail. But you don't have to delve far into the history books to see what has happened to other once-dominant powers.... Great powers rise and fall.... America presents unsettling parallels with the disintegration of Rome—a decline of moral values, a loss of political civility, an overextended military, an inability to control national borders, and the growth of fiscal irresponsibility by the central government. Do these sound familiar?[2]

Historian Niall Ferguson suggests that when an empire falls, its demise comes swiftly, often violently, and almost always without warning: "Empires behave like all complex adaptive systems. They function in apparent equilibrium for some unknowable period. And then, quite abruptly, they collapse."[3]

I have had many conversations with Muslim thinkers, and they believe the fall of the West is already well underway—a result of the decline of Christianity. They tell me that, as Christianity disintegrates, it is leaving a spiritual vacuum in the West. Their extreme form of Islam is already rushing in to fill that void. They predict that Western civilization will, like Rome, continue its steady, gradual decline until it reaches a tipping point of sudden, catastrophic downfall.

One Muslim scholar told me, "Islam spread throughout the Middle East and North Africa by the sword. But Western culture will be handed to us on a platter. The people of the West are led about by their feelings and sentimentality. Their passions rule them. Soft and undisciplined, they are no match for the determined soldiers of Islam. The West will fall into our hands like overripe fruit."

Is there no hope? Are our children and grandchildren condemned to watch our civilization collapse around their ears?

No; there is hope. As the late social critic Charles Krauthammer once observed, "The assumption that somehow there exists some predetermined inevitable trajectory, the result of uncontrollable external forces, is wrong. Nothing is inevitable. Nothing is written. For

America today, decline is not a condition. Decline is a choice."[4]

Ours is the generation that must make that choice. We will choose whether our civilization rises or falls. We must make the wise and godly choice for the sake of our children and grandchildren and generations to come. In these pages, I offer a diagnosis of the madness that is dragging our culture down the slippery slope of decline and collapse—and I offer God's prescription for restoring sanity to this madly careening world. In these pages, we will examine the life-and-death struggle for God's truth in the arenas of the family, the classroom, the government, the media, the church, and individual human souls.

In the final chapter, I will lay out a practical, biblical strategy for becoming agents of change and redemption in this present crisis. I will show how you and I can become people of faith and moral principles, lovingly and persuasively communicating God's message of wholeness to a broken world.

This is no time for fear. This is a time for faith. Trust God for a great harvest as you become His agent of redemption and His witness for the truth of the gospel to your friends, your neighbors, your social media followers, and your world.

God calls you and me to report for duty and make a difference in this present crisis. How will you answer His call?

REMEMBER THE TRUTH

I N FEBRUARY 2020, Baylor University, a private Baptist Christian university in Texas, hosted author/poet Kaitlin Curtice as a chapel speaker. Though a chapel service is a worship service, Curtice's talk was essentially a lecture on identity politics and gender equality. She never cited Scripture or named the name of Jesus. She opened and closed her talk with prayers to "Mother Mystery" instead of the Judeo-Christian God.[1]

Curtice talked about her inner emotional conflict, the result of being raised by a Southern Baptist mother of European ancestry and abandoned at a young age by a father of Potawatomi Native American ancestry. She spoke movingly of the 1838 "Trail of Death" when more than eight hundred Potawatomi people were forcibly removed from Indiana to a reservation in Kansas.[2] She is on a journey, she said, of becoming a person who listens to Mother Earth as she speaks.

She talked about the need to be *woke* (which means being alert to social injustice) and about decolonizing, which she defined as "the work of breaking down systems of colonization. Colonization is the act of taking and erasing indigenous history, culture, and tradition." She spoke of her journey of decolonizing herself: "I am reclaiming who I am, wrestling with all parts of my identity, my white privilege, my native feminism, my spirituality."[3]

It saddens me that Curtice struggles in her identity, that she condemns the faith of the mother who raised her while embracing the "Mother Earth" worldview of the father who abandoned her. Her lecture might have been appropriate for a class on ethnic studies or political science, but hardly for a chapel devotional at a Christian university.

Curtice didn't inspire students to a deeper relationship with God. Her only references to the Christian faith were denunciations of the church. She claimed, for example, that "as a mixed European and Potawatomi woman," her "inner and outer voice has been silenced, especially by the church"—though she didn't explain how the church had "silenced" her.[4] Wasn't she, in fact, paid by a church institution to speak at the chapel service?

But for me, Kaitlin Curtice's most troubling statement was when she said that to be connected to our own spirituality, we have to be connected to the spirituality of others. What does she mean? How should Christians "connect" to the spirituality of non-Christians?

We find similar sentiments in the words of so-called progressive Christians. We hear it in the "love wins" universalism of Rob Bell and the "generous orthodoxy" of Brian McLaren. In context, it becomes clear that Curtice was urging Baylor students to open themselves up to other religions, such as Curtice's pagan reverence for "Mother Earth."[5]

This post-Christian, post-truth world tells us we

should "connect" with other belief systems by embracing them. The Bible calls this idolatry. Yes, Jesus calls us to love *all* people, including people of other faiths. He demonstrated His love toward the Samaritan woman and the pagan Roman centurion.

But Jesus warns us against polluting the pure truth of the Christian faith with the falsehoods of other religions. Jesus declared Himself to be the way, the truth, and the life, and the *only* way to God the Father. "Connecting" with false religions by worshiping God's creation ("Mother Earth") is explicitly forbidden in God's Word.

Near the end of her talk, Curtice said, "My spiritual liberation is tied up with all my spiritual relatives who face oppression.... Are we not working to be liberated together?"[6]

No. True liberation comes not from being "woke," but from the truth of the gospel of Jesus Christ. As Jesus said in John 8, "If you hold to my teaching, you are really my disciples. Then you will know the truth, and the truth will set you free.... So if the Son sets you free, you will be free indeed."[7]

Symbolic Truth

There is a scene in John 2 in which Jesus goes to the temple in Jerusalem, and He looks around and becomes angry. The temple is a house of worship, the house of God—but the greedy religious leaders were making a huge profit by turning the temple courtyard into a giant swap meet. No one could hear the prayers from the temple because the courtyard was filled with vendors and money changers, all hawking their wares and haggling over prices.

So Jesus braided a whip and strode through the courtyard, scattering the coins of the money changers and overturning their tables. He shouted at the sellers of sacrificial animals, "Get these out of here! Stop turning My Father's house into a market!"

> True liberation comes not from being "woke," but from the truth of the gospel of Jesus Christ.

Several years ago, I taught from this passage in an adult Sunday school class. A successful young Christian businessman spoke up and said, "This incident has always bothered me. I think it was pointless for Jesus to clear the temple. Didn't He know that the very next day, all those vendors and money changers would be back in business at the very same spot?"

I was about to reply, but a stay-at-home mom in the class spoke up first. "Sometimes," she said, "it's important to take symbolic action. Jesus knew He couldn't be there to cleanse the temple every day. But He used that moment to send a message to the nation of Israel. With one dramatic act, Jesus showed the nation what He stood for—and He stood for morally, spiritually pure worship to God."

She was right. We sometimes tell ourselves, "What's the use of taking this action? Any good I accomplish is only temporary. Tomorrow, things will be back to normal, and I might as well have done nothing." Satan would like us to become discouraged and defeated so we will never be effective for God. But there is power in symbolic action. There is power in speaking God's truth boldly and without compromise, even when we think it won't do any permanent good.

God has sent us out on a mission to proclaim His truth to the world. He didn't send us out to be successful. He called us to be faithful and obedient. Whether the world responds to our message or ignores us or throws us in prison or crucifies us, we must faithfully proclaim His uncompromised truth—then leave the results with God.

The Transforming Power of Uncompromised Truth

A few years ago, I watched a televised debate between a prominent atheist and a well-known Christian leader. As they talked, I became increasingly alarmed as the Christian leader compromised the claims of Jesus Christ, one by one. He seemed to be trying to win the approval of the atheist—and the studio audience—by watering down the gospel. It was embarrassing. The further this Christian leader retreated from a bold assertion of God's truth, the more the audience booed and heckled him.

> God has sent us out on a mission to proclaim His truth to the world. He didn't send us out to be successful. He called us to be faithful and obedient.

We call the gospel of Jesus Christ, "the good news." But today's post-Christian world does not view the gospel as good news. Our message of salvation through faith in Jesus Christ is not popular in today's world.

Unfortunately, some Christians try to make Jesus more popular by compromising the truth. You cannot convert the world with a weak and compromised gospel.

The message of the kingdom of God won't win any popularity contests. But it is the truth, and we need the courage to defend God's truth boldly and without compromise. We must stop chasing after the approval of this fallen world. Jesus never compromised the truth to win people over. He never soft-pedaled His message. Whenever Jesus introduced the gospel, He always led with the high cost of being His follower. He always presented the gospel in strong, even confrontational terms.

"Enter through the narrow gate," He said in the Sermon on the Mount. "For wide is the gate and broad is the road that leads to destruction, and many enter through it. But small is the gate and narrow the road that leads to life, and only a few find it" (Matt. 7:13–14).

He taught that our love for God must be all-consuming, not lukewarm or halfhearted. "'Love the Lord your God with all your heart and with all your soul and with all your mind.' This is the first and greatest commandment" (Matt. 22:37–38).

He said that being a Christian demanded a radically different way of relating to other people, including our enemies: "But I tell you, love your enemies and pray for those who persecute you" (Matt. 5:44).

Instead of offering promises of endless health and wealth and a Cadillac in the driveway, Jesus promised His followers a life of hardship and servanthood. "Then Jesus said to his disciples, 'Whoever wants to be my disciple must deny themselves and take up their cross and follow me'" (Matt. 16:24).

Jesus didn't "sell" the gospel as if it were merchandise. He violated every rule of good salesmanship. When a man named Nicodemus came to Jesus by night, it was Nicodemus who sounded like a salesman. He approached Jesus with flattery and compliments, a technique straight out of Salesmanship 101: "Rabbi, we know that you are a teacher who has come from God. For no one could perform the signs you are doing if God were not with him" (John 3:2).

Jesus ignored this attempt at flattery and went straight to the heart of the matter, telling Nicodemus that if he wanted to see the kingdom of God, he had to be born again. He boldly and forcefully told Nicodemus the uncompromised truth.

Nicodemus was a member of the elite Pharisee sect, who considered themselves righteous because of all the rituals and rules they kept. Jesus knew He had to penetrate this smug, self-satisfied mindset. His response to Nicodemus was blunt and even shocking: "You must be born again." In other words, following Christ is not just a matter of believing the right doctrines, attending a particular church, or becoming more religious. It involves a complete spiritual transformation. (See John 3:1–24.)

Nicodemus didn't become a follower of Jesus that night. But Jesus had given him a lot to think about—and Nicodemus gave it a lot of thought.

In John 7, Nicodemus makes a second appearance in John's Gospel. There the religious leaders gathered to plot against Jesus. Though Nicodemus was not yet a follower of Jesus, he had become sympathetic to Jesus. When his fellow Pharisees wanted to condemn Jesus to death without a trial, Nicodemus courageously spoke up:

"Does our law condemn a man without first hearing him to find out what he has been doing?" (John 7:51).

The other religious leaders sneered at Nicodemus, saying: "Are you from Galilee, too? Look into it, and you will find that a prophet does not come out of Galilee" (John 7:52).

After the crucifixion of Jesus, Nicodemus made a third appearance in the Gospel of John. He went with Joseph of Arimathea, a wealthy nobleman, to claim the body of Jesus. Nicodemus brought with him a hundred pounds of spices to prepare the body for burial. By this action, he openly and courageously declared himself to be a disciple of Jesus.

Now, here's an intriguing question: When was Nicodemus born again? His spiritual rebirth didn't occur on the night that Jesus told him, "You must be born again." And I don't think Nicodemus was born again when he spoke up in the meeting of the religious leaders.

We don't know the exact moment of conversion experience of Nicodemus. It may be that Nicodemus was there at the foot of the cross during those awful hours of the crucifixion. Perhaps he remembered the words Jesus spoke to him during their late-night visit: "As Moses lifted up the snake in the wilderness, so the Son of Man must be lifted up, that everyone who believes may have eternal life in him" (John 3:14–15). It may be that he was born again right there at the foot of the cross.

One thing is clear: the bold, uncompromised gospel that Jesus proclaimed accomplished its purpose. Nicodemus was transformed—born again. That's the power of God's truth, proclaimed without compromise or hesitation. It's the power to transform lives—and transformed lives change societies and revive dying nations.

Trust Your Feelings?

The Christian faith stands on a firm foundation of truth, sound reasoning, and solid evidence. In Acts 17, the apostle Paul and his companions arrived in Thessalonica and went first to the Jewish synagogue. The Scriptures tell us, "On three Sabbath days he reasoned with them from the Scriptures, explaining and proving that the Messiah had to suffer and rise from the dead" (Acts 17:2–3).

Later, Paul reached the city of Athens and went to Areopagus (Mars Hill), where he addressed the learned scholars and debaters of that city. He proclaimed the gospel to them and explained that Jesus would one day judge the world. Paul concluded, "He has given proof of this to everyone by raising him from the dead" (Acts 17:31). Because Paul preached a rational gospel, rooted in objective evidence and biblical truth, the Holy Spirit drew many of these logically minded, rational Greeks to faith in Jesus Christ.

As the apostle Peter wrote, "Always be prepared to give an answer to everyone who asks you to give the reason for the hope that you have. But do this with gentleness and respect" (1 Pet. 3:15). Our faith is a reasonable faith, founded on objective truth. The truth of God's Word has played a major role in shaping our civilization.

Many historians agree that the Age of Enlightenment began with the 1687 publication of *Principia Mathematica* by the devoutly Christian scientist and mathematician Sir Isaac Newton. He believed that the universe was created by a rational God whose thoughts could be understood not only through Scripture but through the objective observation of God's created order. Newton wrote:

> This most beautiful system of the sun, planets and comets, could only proceed from the counsel and dominion of an intelligent and powerful Being.... This Being governs all things, not as the soul of the world, but as Lord over all: And on account of his dominion he is wont to be called *Lord God* παντοκράτωρ or *Universal Ruler....* The supreme God is a Being eternal, infinite, absolutely perfect.[8]

With such an exalted view of God's truth, Newton provided the intellectual jump start to the period of history we call the Enlightenment. The era of the Enlightenment extolled the virtues of rational scientific inquiry, objective truth, and human liberty and equality. The Enlightenment undermined the authority of monarchies and aristocracies across Europe. Enlightenment ideals inspired colonial Americans to revolt against the British crown and establish a democratic, constitutional government founded on a belief that "all [people] are created equal, that they are endowed by their Creator with certain unalienable Rights, that among these are Life, Liberty and the pursuit of Happiness."[9]

The Enlightenment era was marked by a rapid increase in scientific knowledge, technological and medical advances, increased food production—progress and knowledge that has contributed to the reduction of poverty and suffering and the elevation of human dignity. I firmly believe that it was the combination of the Protestant Reformation (beginning with the publication of Martin Luther's *Ninety-Five Theses* in 1517) and the Enlightenment (beginning with Newton's *Principia Mathematica* in 1687) that created what we now know as Western Civilization.

Ever since the Enlightenment, Western culture has been built on a foundation of reason and objective truth. That foundation began to crumble in the 1960s. During that decade, our culture underwent a radical transformation. An entire generation was profoundly impacted by a new way of looking at reality in which subjective experience was viewed as superior to objective truth. The tipping point occurred in 1967.

That year, Dr. Timothy Leary began touring college campuses with a psychedelic light-and-sound presentation, "The Death of the Mind." He urged an entire generation to destroy their minds with LSD—to "turn on, tune in, and drop out." It was also the year of the "Summer of Love" when waves of hippies gathered in cities across North America and Europe—a vast culture-wide experiment with drugs, sex, and acid rock with a theme (according to *Time* magazine) of "trust your feelings."[10] Also that year, the Beatles made their pilgrimage to the meet the Maharishi Mahesh Yogi, and the most famous rock band in the world went on to promote mysticism and Eastern religion to a generation through their music. These antirational notions spread like the COVID-19 virus: Turn off your mind. Don't trust reason and evidence. Trust your feelings.

Today the Baby Boomers and hippies are all on Social

Security, but they have taught the "trust your feelings" mantra to their children and grandchildren. As a result, succeeding generations have become even more divorced from rational thinking and truth than ever before.

The idea that emotions are more reliable than truth, reason, and evidence is pervasive in the self-help industry. For example, a book was published a few years ago with a chapter called "Trust Your Feelings, Not Your Reasoning." In that chapter, the author wrote, "Don't trust your thinking. It could be warped. Pay attention to your emotions, feelings, and moods, because they are clear indicators of the quality of your thinking, your current level of consciousness....Emotions have their own logic. They are linked to an inner knowing that we can trust."[11]

What poisonous advice! Rational thought may be warped, but emotions are trustworthy? How wise and reliable are the emotions of a person contemplating suicide? Or the husband tempted to cheat on his wife? Or the teenager tempted to give her virginity to her boyfriend? Or the driver venting his road rage at a hundred miles an hour? Or the embittered boy planning a school shooting? Should we tell them, "Trust your feelings"?

God gave us our emotions for a reason. Feelings of joy and love give meaning to our lives. Feelings of anger and fear warn us of danger and protect us from harm. But God never intended that our emotions should rule us. He gave us rational minds so that we could receive His truth and manage our emotions.

A few years before John R. W. Stott went to be with the Lord in 2011, I visited him at his London home. John was Rector of All Souls Church, Langham Place, London, from 1950 to 1975. I met him in 1971, and he became my mentor and friend for many years. During our conversation, we discussed the danger of allowing ourselves to be controlled by emotion instead of reason and truth. "The mind," he said to me at one point, "should be the thermostat which sets the temperature for the emotions."

That's an excellent analogy. If we kept the mind in control of the temperature of our emotions, we would make wiser decisions—and we would save ourselves much grief.

A Cascade of Delusion

In recent years, sociologists have been studying phenomena in our culture that they call "information cascade" and "availability cascade." I believe a better term would be "delusion cascade." A delusion cascade occurs when a false and dangerous idea spreads through a large group of people, becoming a self-reinforcing collective belief.

Here's how it works: One person announces a new idea—usually a simplistic explanation for a frightening and complex situation. Soon a few like-minded people accept the idea and begin repeating it. At first, the new concept may meet resistance and skepticism. But as it is repeated and more people start to accept it, the idea builds a momentum of its own. As the idea spreads by word of mouth, social media, or mainstream media, it creates pressure for people to conform.

When we hear an idea repeated again and again, our need for approval and acceptance begins to overwhelm our discernment and reasoning ability. Instead of asking ourselves, "Is this idea true?" we think, "I don't want people to judge me or reject me! I need to get in step with what everyone else is saying." So the cascade of delusion spreads from person to person and becomes a self-reinforcing lie that significant numbers of people believe.

A prime example of a delusion cascade occurred in April 2020 when someone started a rumor on social media that 5G cell phone towers caused the COVID-19 pandemic. How could cell phone towers cause the spread of disease? There were many theories—each more absurd and irrational than the one before. Some said the virus was a cover story to explain away radiation sickness caused by the towers. Others said cell phone radiation accelerated the growth of the virus. Still others said the cellular waves implanted the virus in human cells.

It was all nonsense, of course—an absurd delusion spread by people who wanted a simple explanation for a frightening global contagion. Several people took it seriously enough to set fire to 5G cellular towers in Great Britain and China—and celebrities, including actor Woody Harrelson and British rap star M.I.A., posted their concerns about the subject on social media.[12]

I believe Satan uses delusion cascades to spread his lies and blind people to the truth. He even implants the delusional notion that objective truth doesn't matter. When people reach a place in their thinking where truth is no longer a relevant or meaningful concept, then their hearts become darkened and impenetrable to the gospel. You cannot persuade a person that Jesus is the way, the truth, and the life (John 14:6) if that person has no respect for truth.

A Post-Truth Church?

Today information comes at us like water gushing from a fire hose. It comes at us from the internet, from twenty-four-hour cable news channels, from social media on our computers and phones. Unfortunately not all information is truth. We all face the challenge of trying to discern the difference between truth and falsehood, between real news and fake news. Even so-called "fact-checking" websites have become propaganda tools for people with a hidden agenda.

Surrounded by so many competing voices, all claiming to be true, many have given up trying to discern truth from falsehood. They say, "You have your truth, and I have mine." They have decided that all opinions are equally valid and that subjective feelings are just as reliable as objective truth and reason. In their confused worldview, it doesn't matter what we believe: "Don't confuse me with facts."

The Barna Group of Ventura, California, has conducted nationwide surveys showing that worldly, anti-Christian beliefs have profoundly infected the Christian community. Reporting on a 2017 study conducted for Summit Ministries, Barna researchers wrote:

> We live in a world of competing ideas and worldviews. In an increasingly globalized and interconnected world, Christians are more aware of (and influenced by) disparate views than ever. But just how much have other worldviews crept into Christians' perspectives? Barna's research shows that only 17 percent of Christians who consider

their faith important and attend church regularly actually have a biblical worldview.[13]

How can this be? Are we becoming a post-truth church in the twenty-first century? How is it possible that *only 17 percent* of serious Christians, regular church-attenders, look at the world through the lens of God's Word? Barna Group researchers went on to explain the definition of a biblical worldview:

[The Barna Group] defines "biblical worldview" as believing that absolute moral truth exists; the Bible is totally accurate in all of the principles it teaches; Satan is considered to be a real being or force, not merely symbolic; a person cannot earn their way into Heaven by trying to be good or do good works; Jesus Christ lived a sinless life on earth; and God is the all-knowing, all-powerful creator of the world who still rules the universe today.[14]

What are the prevailing ideas and worldviews that are reshaping and distorting the beliefs of today's Christians?

Barna Group found that 61 percent of Christians agree with ideas from the New Spirituality movement, which includes influences of Eastern religion, New Age mysticism, and reincarnation. They found that 54 percent of Christians have a postmodern worldview, which is influenced by skepticism toward objective truth, moral relativism, and a pluralistic acceptance of non-Christian religion. The research group found that 38 percent of Christians are sympathetic to some of the teachings of Islam, and 36 percent have adopted a Marxist view (apparently unaware that the Marxist ideology has murdered and enslaved hundreds of millions of people down through history). They also found that 29 percent believe ideas rooted in secularism, which is explicitly anti-Christian and seeks to banish the Christian message from the public square.[15]

We look around us and lament the lostness and blindness of the world. But why is the world lost and blind? Could it be that we who call ourselves Christians have failed to exemplify Jesus Christ to the world? Could it be that we have neglected to hold firmly to the teachings of our Lord? Could it be that we have polluted the gospel purity of Christianity with deceptive ideas from false religions, Marxism, and secularism?

We must cling to the truth of the gospel—the truth that Jesus alone is the way, the truth, and the life. We must never be ashamed of sharing the good news of Jesus Christ with friends, neighbors, and social media acquaintances. We must reject the temptation to dilute and pollute the truth of the gospel to win friendship with this dying world.

As Jesus said, "You are the salt of the earth. But if the salt loses its saltiness, how can it be made salty again? It is no longer good for anything, except to be thrown out and trampled underfoot" (Matt. 5:13). The saltiness Jesus speaks of is His truth exemplified in our lives through both word and deed.

Don't lose your saltiness, my friend. Sprinkle the salty truth of the gospel of Jesus Christ wherever you go.

Headed for a Crash

God's truth can be mocked, ridiculed, ignored, disbelieved, despised, or rejected, but God's truth cannot be destroyed. His truth stands firm even if the world around us collapses into ruin. His truth stands firm even if no human heart on earth believes it. We are free to say no to God's truth, but we cannot bend His truth to our will. God's truth is immovable, unchangeable, and indestructible.

We cannot say to God, "You have your truth, and I have my truth." If our so-called truth does not align perfectly with God's truth, then we are hopelessly self-deceived—and we are in great spiritual danger. Let me suggest an analogy.

One July night in 1999, thirty-eight-year-old John F. Kennedy Jr.—the son of President Kennedy—was piloting his single-engine Piper Saratoga airplane over the Atlantic, from New Jersey to Martha's Vineyard, Massachusetts. His passengers were his wife, Carolyn, and sister-in-law, Lauren Bessette. They were planning to attend the wedding of Rory Elizabeth Kennedy, their cousin.

JFK Jr. had flown this route many times—yet he was only halfway through his instrument training course and had rarely flown at night. This was a moonless night, and a thick haze hid the shore lights. Kennedy could not see the horizon.

The mind and senses can be fooled by the motion of the plane, especially in the dark of night. An airplane's instruments, when properly calibrated, tell us the objective truth. They show whether an aircraft is climbing, descending, or flying level. A pilot who trusts the objective truth of his instruments can't go wrong. But a pilot who trusts his feelings is likely to slip into what pilots call "the graveyard spiral."

A mere twenty miles from his destination, John F. Kennedy Jr. began to doubt his instruments—and he started to trust his feelings. Airport radar showed that his plane was on course for the airstrip—but for some inexplicable reason, he made two turns that took him away from the landing site. Those turns tipped the plane into a graveyard spiral—and the aircraft crashed into the sea, killing everyone aboard.

> **We are free to say no to God's truth, but we cannot bend His truth to our will.**

Investigators concluded that Kennedy experienced "spatial disorientation" and lost his sense of equilibrium and direction. Had he trusted his instruments, he would have arrived safely on the ground.[16] But Kennedy trusted his feelings, not the objective truth of his instruments—and his feelings betrayed him.

Today our nation and our entire culture are flying through the darkness, ignoring the authoritative truth of God's Word—and we, too, are headed for a crash.

RESTORE THE SOUL

I'M GOING TO make you a genuine pizza, the most authentic pizza you've ever tasted. What makes my pizza so authentic? Well, it's all about the right ingredients. I'm sure you're familiar with the so-called pizza they sell in Italian restaurants, with a crust, tomato sauce, mozzarella cheese, and toppings. But that's not real pizza.

I make my authentic pizza with white bread, a thin layer of mayonnaise, a slice of baloney, and I top it off with another slice of bread. *Voilà*! An authentic Michael Youssef pizza.

What's that? What do you mean, it's not a real pizza? What did you call it? A baloney sandwich! My friend, you don't know authentic pizza when you see it.

All right, enough kidding. That little demonstration may seem bizarre, but it perfectly parallels a message we hear again and again in Christian circles today.

There are teachers, preachers, and authors who claim to be Christians, who claim to be preaching the purest and most authentic Christian gospel. Yet they have removed everything that makes the gospel authentically Christian: the reality of sin, the depravity of man, the virgin birth, the atoning death of Christ, the resurrection, justification by grace through faith. For more than two thousand years, these doctrines have defined what Christianity is.

But this new crop of teachers, preachers, and authors would have us believe that what we've been taught is not "authentic Christianity." They have replaced orthodox Christian teachings with "narrative" and "postmodern theology" and "social justice" and political activism. They trade the "pizza" of authentic Christianity for a lot of baloney.

What's more, they are telling us the church has been wrong throughout all two thousand years of Christian history. Orthodox Christianity is wrong, the Bible is wrong, and Jesus is wrong. This pseudo-Christian baloney they've devised in their imagination is the only "real" Christianity. You may think I'm exaggerating. I'm not.

Read the words of one of the early popularizers of progressive or postmodern Christianity, retired Episcopal bishop John Shelby Spong. He wrote a series of books that promoted a new version of "Christianity"—a version without sin or guilt or any need for Jesus to die on the cross to save us. He told an interviewer:

> The thing that bothers me most about the Christian church today is that we spend our time confirming people in their own sense of wretchedness. You can't go to church without praying ten or fifteen times for God to have mercy on you. You can't sing "Amazing Grace" without reminding yourself that the reason God's grace is amazing is it saves a wretch like you. This self-denigration stuff—Jesus

died for my sins—is nothing but a guilt message.
That's the thing we've got to get out from under.
That's not Christianity.[1]

Do you see? Bishop Spong is telling us that biblical Christianity isn't real Christianity, that pizza isn't pizza, and that his baloney is the real deal.

But Spong is wrong. A Christianity that sings "Amazing Grace" is *real* Christianity. We *are* wretched, we *are* lost in sin, and Jesus *died on the cross* to save us from our sins. Some narrow-minded preachers or theologians did not invent these doctrines. They come straight from the lips of Jesus the Master. He is the One who originated Christianity, and He tells us we are wretched and that we desperately needed Him to die for our sins.

In the Sermon on the Mount, Jesus said, "If you, then, *though you are evil*, know how to give good gifts to your children, how much more will your Father in heaven give good gifts to those who ask him!" (Matt. 7:11, emphasis added).

To whom was Jesus talking? Not the scribes and Pharisees. He was talking to His followers, to people who had sought Him out to hear Him preach on the mountainside. In the original Greek, He called these followers Πονηροὶ, "evil," the same word the New Testament routinely uses to describe Satan. Yes, we are wretched, we are sinful, we are evil—and that is why the lyrics of "Amazing Grace" are so true.

As Jesus reminds us, we are capable of doing good things and giving good gifts—but that doesn't change the fact that we are evil and wretched and lost in our sins. That's why we need a Savior—and that's a foundational truth of Christianity.

Any teaching that says differently is baloney.

True Freedom

Why have many so-called Christians abandoned the teachings of Jesus and the Bible? Why do they deny two thousand years of orthodox Christian doctrine and tradition?

I believe it's because many of today's false teachers want to be accepted and admired by the world. They don't want to be lumped in with all those "rigid," "narrow-minded," "intolerant" evangelical Christians. They want to be admired for their "enlightened," "open-minded," "inclusive" approach to religion.

These false teachers often label themselves progressive Christians or "postmodern Christians" or "post-evangelical Christians" or "the emerging church." It sometimes takes a great deal of discernment to distinguish a progressive Christian from an orthodox, Bible-believing, evangelical Christian. Why? Because progressive Christians use the same words we use—but with very different meanings.

- Progressive Christians say they believe *the Bible is divinely inspired*, but they don't mean it is the Spirit-breathed, infallible Word of God. They mean it is inspired the same way the plays of Shakespeare and the poems of Emily Dickinson are "inspired."

- Progressive Christians say they believe that
  God is love. So do we, because God loved
  the world so much that He gave His only
  Son to die on the cross for us. But progressive Christians don't believe the cross
  is an expression of God's love. Instead,
  they teach that a loving God would never
  punish sinners or judge sin or condemn an
  unrepentant, unbelieving sinner to hell.

- Progressive Christians say they believe in
  the authority of Scripture. So do we. But
  they claim that Scripture has been misun-
  derstood and misapplied for the last two
  thousand years of Christian history. They
  are the first Christians in history to understand what the Bible means, and which
  parts we should obey or ignore.

- Progressive Christians say they believe in
  the *resurrection.* So do we. But if you press
  them about whether they affirm that the
  resurrection was a literal, physical, historical event, they will tell you that the resurrection of Jesus is a powerful spiritual
  metaphor, and a metaphor doesn't have to
  be literal and historical to convey important truth.

And on and on. You can carry on quite a long conversation with a progressive Christian, and they will
speak the same vocabulary as you, and you will seem
to be on the same wavelength. But if you carry on the

conversation long enough and if you ask the right questions, you'll eventually discover that you might as well be shouting from different planets. Their "Christianity" is not the Christianity of the Bible, and it is certainly not the Christianity of Jesus the Messiah.

Our fallen, dying culture loves and approves of progressive Christianity, because this baloney form of "Christianity" makes no moral judgments against sin and is perfectly aligned with a worldly, secular-left political agenda. For example, a recent headline on the left-leaning news and opinion website *The Daily Beast* proclaimed, "They Have Faith Their Church Will Change." In this profile of progressive Christians, journalist Brandon Withrow wrote:

> They're young, liberal, LGBTQ+, pro-choice, feminist, science loving, climate change accepting, and immigrant welcoming. They're evangelicals.
>
> No, this is not a report from an alternate universe, where history took a different turn. This is about a growing rift in the evangelical continuum…that's forced some progressive evangelicals to part ways with the name. Just this week, co-founder of the progressive Red Letter Christian movement, Tony Campolo, told Premier that "A lot of people who are evangelical in their theology do not want to be called 'evangelicals' anymore." Being evangelical in the United States means "you're anti-gay, you're anti-women, you're pro-war."[2]

If you want to be approved by this dying world, it's easy. Simply abandon the foundational truths of Christianity:

the Bible is the Word of God, we are saved by grace through faith in the atoning death of Jesus Christ, Jesus arose and is seated at the right hand of God the Father, and He is coming again to judge the world. Then replace the Christian gospel with a secular-left agenda of identity politics, climate change, unrestricted abortion and infanticide, LGBTQ politics, Darwinism, and on and on. Then tell the world, "This secular-left political agenda is *real* Christianity—those two-thousand-year-old dogmas from the Bible are fake."

As the apostle James warned, "You adulterous people, don't you know that friendship with the world means enmity against God? Therefore, anyone who chooses to be a friend of the world becomes an enemy of God" (Jas. 4:4). If you adopt a secular social and political agenda, the world will love you. You'll have many friends in this fallen and dying world. But the price you will pay is a state of enmity between you and God.

One leader in the progressive Christian movement has condemned what he calls the "gospel of saving individual souls from hell."[3] In its place, he advocates a "gospel" focused on political action, social justice, environmentalism, and the gay rights agenda. He is offering us a false choice: either we preach the gospel of salvation by grace through faith in Christ, as proclaimed in the Bible, or we promote a gospel of social action. This claim ignores all Christian history, which shows that those who preach the uncompromised gospel of salvation have always made the most significant impact for good in society. As C. S. Lewis wrote:

A continual looking forward to the eternal world is not (as some modern people think) a form of escapism or wishful thinking, but one of the things a Christian is meant to do. It does not mean that we are to leave the present world as it is. If you read history you will find that the Christians who did most for the present world were just those who thought most of the next. The Apostles themselves, who set on foot the conversion of the Roman Empire, the great men who built up the Middle Ages, the English Evangelicals who abolished the Slave Trade, all left their mark on Earth, precisely because their minds were occupied with Heaven. It is since Christians have largely ceased to think of the other world that they have become so ineffective in this. Aim at Heaven and you will get earth "thrown in"; aim at earth and you will get neither.[4]

It's true. For example, in the years before the American Civil War, the most significant social reformers and abolitionists were soul-winning evangelical preachers like Charles Finney and Theodore Weld. Instead of abandoning the gospel of salvation of souls, we desperately need to restore the biblical gospel to its rightful, central place in the ministry of the church.

Jesus said, "If you hold to my teaching, you are really my disciples" (John 8:31). These so-called progressive Christians do not hold to the Lord's teaching. They openly reject everything Jesus said about His blood, His death, and His atonement for sin. They openly reject His claim to be the way, the truth, the life—the *only* way to God the Father. To them, Jesus is *a* way, but not *the* way.

Having rejected all these teachings of Jesus, they still want to be seen as Christians. Jesus said we can't have it both ways. Rejecting His teachings leads to slavery. Holding to His teachings sets us free. Satan desires to keep us in slavery. He wants to bind us in chains of doubt and delusion. The "gospel" of the progressive Christians is a false gospel that leads to spiritual enslavement.

Jesus warned, "Watch out for false prophets. They come to you in sheep's clothing, but inwardly they are ferocious wolves. By their fruit you will recognize them. Do people pick grapes from thornbushes, or figs from thistles? Likewise, every good tree bears good fruit, but a bad tree bears bad fruit" (Matt. 7:15–17).

Satan has already infiltrated the evangelical church, sending among us wolves who look and sound and act like sheep. Once they are inside the fold, mingling with the sheep, they become wolves in every way. They pounce, devour, and destroy—and they do so from within the church, disguised as sheep.

In Psalm 11:3, David asks, "When the foundations are being destroyed, what can the righteous do?" Today false teachers who claim to be Christians attack the foundations of Christianity. Wolves disguised as sheep are devouring the church from within.

Stand Firm for the Truth

In the early years of The Church of The Apostles, the well-known pastor of a thriving megachurch visited our little congregation and listened as I preached. After the service, he critiqued my sermon. "Michael," he said, "I hope you'll take this criticism in the spirit in which I intend it. I want to see your church grow, and I know you want that too. But your church will never grow if you keep preaching sermons like the one I heard today. All this preaching about sin and confession and repentance is too negative. If you want to have a large church ministry that has a major impact on the community, you need to preach happy, positive sermons that make people feel good about themselves."

I considered his advice. I wondered, "What if he's right? After all, our church is tiny and struggling while his church is large and thriving."

But soon I felt God speaking to me. He said, "Michael, I would rather you reach heaven with a handful of people who came to saving faith through your uncompromised preaching than have you entertain tens of thousands who will curse you from hell because you compromised My truth."

That day, I made a vow to God that as long as He would give me breath, I would proclaim His uncompromised truth. Whether people loved me or hated me, praised me or loathed me, I would hold fast to the teachings of Jesus, the truth of God's Word.

We dare not be casual about attacks on God's truth—especially when those attacks come from within the church, from people who call themselves Christians. Truth and freedom are linked. God's truth in our lives, expressed through the fruit of the Holy Spirit, leads to love, joy, peace, forbearance, kindness, goodness, faithfulness, gentleness, and self-control. (See Galatians 5:22–23.) The rejection of God's truth leads to hatred, envy, anxiety, resentment, cruelty, sin, faithlessness, brutality, and addiction. In short, it leads to enslavement to sin. That's why Paul tells us, "Now the Lord is the Spirit, and where the Spirit of the Lord is, there is freedom" (2 Cor. 3:17).

Freedom comes from clinging tightly to the teachings of Jesus. Every action we take, every decision we make, should be based on the truth of His gospel. Every business deal we make has consequences for God's truth. Have we demonstrated integrity and truthfulness in this business deal? Will this transaction honor God, or will it stain our testimony?

Every financial decision we make has ramifications for God's truth. Should we spend our income on material things and entertainment? It might be more honoring to God to invest a significant amount of our earnings in expanding the kingdom of God, to save some of our income prudently, or to pay down our debts and live more frugally, so we can give more to God in the future. We should examine all these decisions in light of the truth of the gospel.

Every political decision has consequences for God's truth. Should we vote for the politician who promises to give us the most stuff—or the politician who has a track record of integrity, godly priorities, and responsible government? Should we vote for a particular ballot initiative or against it? How would Jesus urge us to vote?

God's truth impacts every aspect of our lives. The teachings of Jesus serve as guardrails for our thoughts, words, and actions. Between the guardrails of the Lord's teaching, there is great freedom. Outside those guardrails, there is enslavement.

The infinite wisdom and power of God are available to us through prayer and His Word. Ask God to strengthen you as you contend for His truth at home, at work, and in your community. Ask God to empower you to witness boldly for His truth. Pray that He will give you the wisdom and discernment to resist the alluring falsehoods of progressive Christianity and other forms of apostasy so prevalent today. If you hold to the teachings of Jesus, then you will know His truth, and His truth will set you free.

The world exerts constant pressure on us to conform. It is continually trying to squeeze us into its mold. The teachings of Jesus are our only defense against the pressure of our dying, godless society.

- Our culture says that Jesus is one of many ways to God. But Jesus said, "I am the way and the truth and the life. No one comes to the Father except through me" (John 14:6).

- Our culture says that although Jesus was a good moral teacher, He never rose from the dead—and neither will we. But Jesus said, "I am the resurrection and the life. The one who believes in me will live, even though they die" (John 11:25).

- Our culture says that Jesus taught us how to live a good life here on earth, not how to be "saved" or have "eternal life." But Jesus said, "For God so loved the world that he gave his one and only Son, that whoever believes in him shall not perish but have eternal life" (John 3:16).

Stand firm on these truths. Don't budge from these truths. Be gracious and kind when you share these truths with the people around you, but don't let anyone talk you out of them. Don't expect people to believe you or applaud you when you hold fast to the teachings of Jesus. He calls us to stand firm for His gospel—but we shouldn't be surprised when the world rejects God's truth. We should expect to be persecuted for it.

Don't Be Afraid

In late December 2019, doctors in Wuhan, China, became alarmed over an outbreak of a disease that appeared to be an unknown form of pneumonia. One of those doctors, a thirty-four-year-old ophthalmologist named Li Wenliang, had been treating a patient with mysterious symptoms. When he read a report from the emergency department at Central Hospital of Wuhan, he realized that a new and dangerous strain of coronavirus was spreading in Wuhan.

> We shouldn't be surprised when the world rejects God's truth. We should expect to be persecuted for it.

Dr. Li posted a message to a private WeChat group for his medical school classmates. He urged his friends to inform their family members to take precautions against this new virus. Someone posted his warnings on the Chinese internet.

On January 3, 2020, police from the Wuhan Public Security Bureau arrested him and took him to the police station. They gave him a written warning that condemned him for making false statements on the internet. They also warned him that he was dangerously close to being prosecuted and imprisoned.

Dr. Li was a father with a five-year-old son and a pregnant wife. He didn't want to put his young family in jeopardy, so he agreed not to post any more information about the virus, and he quietly returned to his work at the hospital.

While working at the hospital, he contracted the virus and became seriously ill. On January 31, knowing he might not have long to live, Dr. Li published a letter on state-controlled social media. Before the Communist government could take his message down, his post went viral, and thousands of Chinese citizens captured screenshots of it.

In his letter, Dr. Li described his experience at the police station, when officials intimidated him into silence. Their threats worked for a while, but after Dr. Li became desperately sick, he realized he needed to speak the truth without fear. In his letter, he questioned why the police had silenced him and other doctors who had warned of the disease. The repressive action against the doctors had only served to increase the spread of this life-threatening disease.

A short time after his letter was posted online, Dr. Li told an interviewer, "It's not so important to me if I'm vindicated or not. What's more important is that everyone knows the truth."

A few days later, on February 7, 2020, the virus claimed his life.

In the wake of his death, Dr. Li Wenliang was widely hailed as a martyr for truth. News of his demise prompted more than half a billion posts on social media, some memorializing his sacrifice, and others demanding the right of free speech in Communist China.

Stories also circulated that Dr. Li was a Christian—although it's difficult to know if those stories are true. We do know that Dr. Li posted regularly in a Christian chat room. At the very least, he was inquiring into Christianity—and he may well have been a born-again believer.[5]

Dr. Li Wenliang is a role model for you and me. When the police hauled him to the police station and threatened him with arrest, he obeyed out of fear for himself and his family. But then something happened. Dr. Li contracted the virus. He realized he might not have long to live. As he faced this life-and-death crisis, his fear vanished. In those moments, only one thing mattered to him: "that everyone knows the truth."

Someone once said, "God does not require you to win, but he does require you to fight." Dr. Li chose to fight until his dying breath.

When God calls us to dare great things for Him, we have a choice: we can step out in faith, or we can shrink back in fear. When the world seeks to persecute us and silence our witness, will we fight or fold?

Friendship with the world is enmity with God. If we are not at odds with our culture, then we are at odds with God. The apostle John tells us those who do not acknowledge Jesus "are from the world and therefore speak from the viewpoint of the world, and the world listens to them. We are from God, and whoever knows God listens to us; but whoever is not from God does not listen to us. This is how we recognize the Spirit of truth and the spirit of falsehood" (1 John 4:5–6).

Don't be afraid of the world and its persecution. Don't be timid or ashamed of the gospel. When you feel God prompting you to speak up and challenge falsehood, take a moment to breathe a brief prayer: "Lord, please give me Your words to speak. Amen!"

Take with you these encouraging, motivating words of Paul: "Be on your guard; stand firm in the faith; be courageous; be strong" (1 Cor. 16:13).

He Restores My Soul

For centuries, believers have turned to one resource in times of crisis and fear—Psalm 23, a psalm of King David.

> The LORD is my shepherd, I lack nothing. He makes me lie down in green pastures, he leads me beside quiet waters, he refreshes my soul. He guides me along the right paths for his name's sake. Even though I walk through the darkest valley, I will fear no evil, for you are with me; your rod and your staff, they comfort me. You prepare a table before me in the presence of my enemies. You anoint my head with oil; my cup overflows. Surely your goodness and love will follow me all the days of my life, and I will dwell in the house of the LORD forever.

The words the New International Version translates "Even though I walk through the darkest valley" are (in my view) more beautifully rendered in the King James Version: "Yea, though I walk through the valley of the shadow of death." The global COVID-19 pandemic of 2020 was a reminder that the entire world is truly a "valley of the shadow of death." An invisible virus traveled around the globe threatening lives in every nation on earth. All around the world, people lived in fear of being invaded by this unseen enemy.

The COVID-19 crisis reminded us that death could come from anywhere, at any time, without warning. The moment we were conceived, we began a process that must ultimately end in death.

But God does not want us to live in fear of death. Even though we walk through the valley of the shadow of death, we fear no evil. Why? Because God is with us, comforting us, encouraging us, providing for us, and guarding us even in the presence of our enemies.

Jesus, the Good Shepherd, restores our souls and leads us into paths of true righteousness. If we hold tightly to His teaching—all of it, without compromise—we will know the truth, and the truth will set us free. We will walk in paths of righteousness, giving glory to His name. Then we will not fall prey to any false gospels or any worldly agenda disguised as "Christianity." God will use our crises and afflictions to mold our lives so that we become reflections of God's love and grace to this dying world.

God is not the author of heartache and tragedy, but He excels in using tough times for our growth and benefit— and for His glory. No one escapes adversity. Grief and sorrow are inevitable in this fallen world. But we do not have to live with defeat and discouragement. Even amid threats and persecution from God's enemies, He anoints our head with oil, and our cup of blessing overflows.

You may be thinking, "Michael, you don't know my circumstances. You don't understand the opposition and pressure I'm facing in my workplace, on my campus, in my neighborhood." You're right; I don't know what you are going through. But Jesus knows, and He understands perfectly. He is the Good Shepherd who comforts and guides you.

Jesus, our Shepherd, was rejected, betrayed, crowned with thorns, and crucified. If you are feeling alone in your crisis of suffering, look to Jesus. He is walking through the valley alongside you. No matter how dark your life becomes, He understands and will lead you through the valley. He will quench your thirst beside still waters. He will carry you when you are broken and weak.

Because the Good Shepherd leads you, there is nothing to fear—not even death itself. His goodness and mercy follow you throughout this life, and you will dwell in the house of the Lord forever.

Our Shepherd is like no other. He was even willing to die for us, His sheep. Jesus tells us, "I am the good shepherd. The good shepherd lays down his life for the sheep" (John 10:11). He is never off the clock. He continually cares, provides, and watches over us. When the secularists, atheists, hedonists, false teachers, apostates, and other worldly forces come after us to persecute us for our faithfulness to Christ, the Good Shepherd will be with us, giving us courage and comfort, and restoring our souls.

Sheep have only one responsibility: to follow the shepherd. Don't be a fearful or wayward sheep. Don't fear the wolves that hunt you. Cast your anxieties on the Good

Shepherd. He knows the way through the valley of the shadow of death.

He has walked through this valley before, and He cares for you.

REVITALIZE THE FAMILY

LORIDA PASTOR KEN Whitten tells a story about his daughter Tara, the oldest of his four children. Whitten and his wife, Ginny, raised their children to live according to uncompromised biblical principles. One of those principles was that they would never watch an R-rated movie.

When Tara was a college junior, her instructor gave the class an assignment that involved watching an R-rated movie and being tested on its content. Tara told her professor she could not view the film because it would violate her moral convictions. The professor told her she had to watch the movie or receive a zero for the assignment. Tara said, "I'll have to take the zero."

Seeing that Tara meant business, the professor offered to let her write a paper instead. So Tara wrote a ten-page paper called "Proverbs 31: A Godly Woman." Not only did the professor give her an A, but she received the only A in the class.[1]

A godly family that refuses to compromise God's truth is a powerful witness to the world and a potent force for transforming society. Tragically families are under assault in our culture as never before. As families disintegrate, children pay the price. Messages that attack faith and values bombard Christian kids. Their teachers and the media tell them there's no such thing as objective truth, that they are nothing but highly evolved animals, that it's normal and healthy to yield to their most basic and self-centered impulses.

Parents are increasingly operating on feelings instead of biblical principles and God's truth. Instead of raising their kids in the nurture and admonition of the Lord, parents have surrendered to their children's emotions—including childish anger and juvenile rage. When Edward VIII, the Duke of Windsor, visited the United States in 1957, *Life* magazine recorded his remark that "The thing that impresses me most about America is the way parents obey their children."[2] If that was his observation in 1957, imagine what he would say today!

The family is God's idea. In Genesis, God said that the plan for marriage is that "a man leaves his father and mother and is united to his wife, and they become one flesh" (Gen. 2:24), and He told Adam and Eve to be fruitful and multiply and subdue the earth. The Bible states clearly, from beginning to end, that the family is the most important element in society and the backbone of a nation. If we weaken the family, we erode our cultural foundation. If the family disintegrates, the collapse of society is sure to follow. We are seeing this in our own culture today.

There is a high price to be paid for weakening the family—a cost measured in trillions of dollars and millions of shattered lives. The United States is incurring a mountain of debt in no small part because of the breakdown of the family. Broken families place a huge financial burden on the welfare state. Broken families lead to crime, drug abuse, homelessness, and poverty, which impose a massive strain on the health care system, law enforcement, and prisons. Measured in dollars alone, the cost to society of the breakdown of the family is staggering. Add the toll of human misery, and the price simply cannot be measured. Destroy the family and, as sure as night follows day, you will destroy society.

After studying the breakdown of families in America, the Heritage Foundation found:

- High-crime neighborhoods are densely populated by fatherless families.

- The rate of violent crime committed by teens corresponds to the number of families without fathers.

- Neighborhoods with more religiously observant families have lower crime rates.

- Even in high-crime neighborhoods, 90 percent of children from stable, intact homes do not become delinquents.

- The best buffers against a life of crime are a mother's affectionate love and a father's involvement and authority.[3]

God did not merely design the Christian family as a shield to protect children from worldly influences. He created the Christian family as a beachhead, an invasion force with a mission of retaking satanically occupied society for the kingdom of God. As Christian social critic Rodney Clapp observes in *A Peculiar People*, "The church sees family life as a great good. But the Christian family does not live, as some families in some cultures have, to perpetuate a name or preserve a nation-state by providing taxpayers and soldiers. The Christian family is defined by its action as an agent of the church to witness to the truth of the kingdom of God."[4]

It's vitally important that Christian parents wage spiritual warfare against this fallen culture, battling for the souls of their children. But defending our children's souls is not enough. We must actively and intentionally send our children out into the world as agents of spiritual and moral transformation. One of the most effective responses we can make to this present crisis is to revitalize our families to take territory for the kingdom of God.

Run to the Battle

A few years ago, a concerned father named Gil Reavill wrote a book about how our sex-drenched culture is destroying the lives of our children. He warned that we are failing our kids by allowing them to be exposed to "the world of commercial sex" through the internet, TV, movies, music, print media, and more. He was appalled at the sexually charged media to which his teenage daughter had already been exposed.

"The young," he wrote, "are powerless, voiceless, totally reliant on adults.... The boundaries of their world have been repeatedly breached, many times by people interested in making money and dismissive of all other considerations. All too often, our children are exposed to the loud, frenzied, garish spectacle of adult sexuality. They get their faces rubbed in it."[5]

A concerned Christian parent could have easily written those words—but Gil Reavill doesn't claim to be a Christian. He has made his career *within the commercial sex industry* since the early 1980s. He has written for *Playboy, Penthouse, Maxim,* and publications with names so obscene I won't repeat them here. His book is called *Smut: A Sex-Industry Insider (and Concerned Father) Says Enough Is Enough.*

What changed Reavill's perspective on porn? Becoming a parent. To Gil Reavill, smut was merely a way to make a lot of money—until he became a father. As his daughter grew up, he realized that the porn industry was a threat to her—a threat too pervasive to be avoided. With regret, he recalled all the arguments he used to make when people complained about porn: "If you don't like it, don't read it." "If it offends you, change the channel." "No one is forcing you to watch."

He realized that the pornography industry had created a phenomenon that had never existed before. He called it "the unchangeable channel." He wrote, "The 'off' switch doesn't work anymore. Our culture has been collectively hotwired."[6]

The internet is a wonderful invention for communication, news, information, entertainment, and commerce. But pornographers are always the first to exploit any new technology, from videotape to DVDs to the internet to virtual reality. Godlessness and corruption are all around us—but that's no excuse for yielding to our worst sexual impulses, or for leaving our children vulnerable to predators.

Every internet-connected device is a doorway to an entire world of soul-destroying images and ideas. If you allow your child to sit unmonitored in front of a computer, tablet, or smartphone screen, you are throwing your child's soul to the wolves. In addition to all the good things the World Wide Web has to offer, it is a gathering place for satanists, pornographers, pedophiles, and other threats to your family. If you would not leave your child alone in the middle of a busy freeway, you should not leave your child unsupervised in front of a computer screen.

Let's renew our commitment to building moral guardrails around our private behavior, our sacred marriage relationships, our homes, and our children. If pornography is a habit or addiction or temptation in your life, take steps to regain your moral purity. Ask trusted friends to hold you accountable. Install software on your computer that sends regular reports on your internet usage to a trusted friend. If necessary, unplug your computer and your phone from the internet. This is a matter of spiritual life and death, so take radical action.

A seemingly minor sin can lead to death and destruction. We see this principle in the life of King David. The Scriptures tell us, "In the spring, at the time when kings go off to war, David sent Joab out with the king's men and the whole Israelite army. They destroyed the Ammonites and besieged Rabbah. But David remained in Jerusalem. One evening David got up from his bed and walked around on the roof of the palace. From the roof he saw a woman bathing. The woman was very beautiful" (2 Sam. 11:1–2).

David was supposed to be on the battlefield, but he

was on his palace rooftop instead. He had too much time on his hands, and as the king, he was accountable to no one. He was much like a man today, sitting at his computer, coming upon a pornographic website. David looked, he lusted, and he rationalized: "It doesn't hurt to look, does it?"

The moment he surrendered to his lustful impulses, he set in motion a chain of events that would lead to murder and devastation. First, he entertained fantasies about the woman. Then he acted on his thoughts, and he sent for the woman, whose name was Bathsheba. Then he committed adultery with her—and she became pregnant.

Step by step, he descended into a maelstrom of sin until he was in too deep to climb out. Bathsheba's husband, a soldier named Uriah, had been out on the battlefield for months—the battlefield where David should have been. David realized that, as soon as Bathsheba gave birth, everyone would know the baby was not Uriah's. David could imagine the front-page headlines in the *Jerusalem Post*: "Bathshebagate Scandal: King Caught in Love Nest!"

So King David devised a cover-up. He tried to get Uriah to come home on furlough and spend the night with Bathsheba. But Uriah had such a strong sense of duty to his king and his fellow soldiers that he refused to enjoy sexual relations with his wife while his men were on the battlefield.

David's attempt to cover up his sin was foiled. So he arranged for the murder of Uriah. At David's command, the men of Uriah's unit withdrew from him during battle, leaving him alone to face the enemy. As a result, faithful, honest, loyal Uriah was slain, betrayed by the king he nobly served.

The Scriptures tell us that "the thing David had done displeased the LORD" (2 Sam. 11:27). God sent the prophet Nathan to confront the king. When David's crime was exposed, he repented in deep sorrow—but by then, his sin had caused enormous harm that could never be undone. King David's seemingly "minor" sin of lust had borne the bitter fruit of adultery scandal, murder, and shame. It's not surprising that David's family fell apart.

We cannot lead our children to a place where we have never been. If we want them to live according to biblical principles, then we have to live by those principles ourselves. We cannot allow "a little lust" or "a little pornography" to gain a foothold in our lives. The stakes are too high.

A Christian Parent's Worst Nightmare

In his book *Twice Adopted*, Michael Reagan, the son of President Ronald Reagan, told a story that is every parent's worst nightmare. Michael's parents divorced when he was three. His mother—Academy Award–winning actress Jane Wyman—sent Michael to boarding school when he was five. And Michael only got to see his father every other weekend.

When Michael was seven, his mother sent him to a day camp operated by a man named Don who had great rapport with children. Don knew that Michael was a lonely boy whose parents were divorced—a boy, in Michael's own words, who was "emotionally needy, emotionally empty and emotionally vulnerable." Starved for attention, Michael sought Don's approval. "I set out," he recalled, "to prove that I was the best at trampolining, the best at somersaults and back flips, the best at sports like baseball and football." Don gave Michael the attention he craved and won the boy's trust. "Don was lavish with compliments," Michael wrote, "and I ate them up."

One day, Don said, "Mike, you want to do something to make me feel good?" Michael said yes. It didn't occur to him that Don was a sexual predator who would do bad things to young boys. From that day forward, Don molested young Michael repeatedly, day after day. He took indecent pictures of the boy and used them for blackmail, saying, "Wouldn't your mom like to have a copy of that picture?"

> We cannot lead our children to a place where we have never been. If we want them to live according to biblical principles, then we have to live by those principles ourselves.

"I really didn't know I was a victim," Michael recalled. "I didn't learn until years later, until I was well into adulthood, that everything I had been feeling—my guilt, my self-hate, my anger, my fear—is common to nearly all sexually exploited children. I thought I was the bad person. I didn't understand that I was the wounded one."

The guilt and terror that this child molester inflicted on young Michael would torment him long into adulthood. Michael blamed and hated God, and felt that God was punishing him unfairly by sending this monster into his life. He asked God, "Why are you doing this to me? What did I ever do to you?"

Michael was in his thirties when his father ran for president. He lived in constant fear, imagining that the awful photos Don had taken might become public. Even after his father was inaugurated, those fears continued to haunt him.

In 1987, as Michael was working on his autobiography, *On the Outside Looking In*, he realized he had to tell the story of being molested as a boy. Thirty-five years had passed, and it was time to break his silence. But first he had to tell his mother, Jane Wyman, and his father and stepmother, Ronald and Nancy Reagan.

Michael's mother was terribly hurt to hear how Michael had suffered with this secret for so many years. She blamed herself. "Michael," she said, "if only I hadn't sent you to that day camp—"

But Michael didn't blame her, and he told her not to blame herself. "How could she have known?" he wrote. "Mom thought she had put me in a safe place. She couldn't teach me how to throw a baseball or a football, so she trusted someone who could.... [Don] seemed like a safe and caring man—the kind of guy you would trust on sight."[7]

Next, Michael went to his father's Santa Barbara ranch during a family retreat. He took his father and Nancy aside, and with tears streaming down his face, he told them about being molested as a child. Michael's father was so furious that he wanted to track the man down and beat him with his own fists—even though he was the sitting president of the United States.

In the 1990s, Michael appeared on a live daytime TV talk show to tell his story. During the show, a viewer called the show and said that he, too, had been molested by Don. The caller had told his father, his father had called the police—and Don spent time in prison for his crimes. But, the caller said, after his release, Don moved to another state where he continued to victimize young boys.

What lessons can we learn from Michael Reagan's early life?

First, no child is immune from danger. If the son of Ronald Reagan and Jane Wyman could be targeted by a predator, then no child is safe. There are many spiritual dangers that threaten our children, from sexual predators to ungodly friends to harmful influences on the internet and in entertainment media to destructive indoctrination in the public schools. Many of the dangers our children face are like wolves in sheep's clothing. Michael's mother trusted Don, the day camp director, because he was engaging, charming, and likable, little realizing that he was plotting to destroy young Michael's soul.

Second, make sure you know who your children are with and what they are doing at all times. Get to know their teachers and coaches well. Get to know their friends. Know who your kids are calling and texting. Make sure you know what's in the video games they play, the shows they watch, and the music they listen to. Make sure you know what your children are being taught in school.

Third, talk to your children—and really listen to them. Look for signs that they are troubled, unhappy, withdrawn, destructive, angry, or fearful. Ask questions and let them know you are deeply interested in their lives. Tell them you love them and you're proud of them. Give them your attention and plenty of hugs.

Fourth, pray *with* your children and pray *for* your children. Pray that they hold on to the faith you have taught them throughout their childhood. The teen years are filled with pressures, temptations, dangerous influences, and seesawing emotions. Give them the rock-solid truth of God's Word to hang on to through the difficult teenage years. Read God's Word together at the family altar.

Fifth, persevere. When your children enter those turbulent teenage years, persist in loving them through it. Tell them about your teenage years, the doubts and emotions and turmoil you went through. Let them know that you got through it by God's grace, and so will they. You may think they aren't listening, and that you have lost your influence with them—but trust me, they're observing you closely.

Teenagers will test their limits—but they are also testing *you* and watching how you respond. They'll argue with everything you say and call you "old-fashioned" and "clueless"—but they'll file away your wisdom for future reference. They'll ponder it and consider it—even though they may never admit it.

Whether your children are preschoolers, high schoolers, or grown adults, you never stop being their parent. Be vigilant and involved. Lift them up to the Lord again and again throughout the day—and throughout their lives. God didn't let go of Michael Reagan, and He won't let go of your children.

An Inheritance From the Lord

Christians often quote the words of Psalm 127:3, which says, "Children are a heritage from the LORD, offspring a reward from him." That is a blessed truth, and every believing parent knows it. But when we quote this verse out of context, we miss out on a deeper truth embedded in these words.

The author of Psalm 127 is King Solomon, the son of David. Before Solomon could say that children are an inheritance from the Lord, he first had to lay the foundation for that statement, which he does in verses 1–2: "Unless the LORD builds the house, the builders labor in vain. Unless the LORD watches over the city, the guards stand watch in vain. In vain you rise early and stay up late, toiling for food to eat—for he grants sleep to those he loves."

Before we can say that children are an inheritance from the Lord, the Lord must build the house. It is the Lord who must build our families.

Psalm 127 is beautifully expressive Hebrew poetry. But beneath this psalm's graceful words is an indictment, a rebuke to the lifestyle of many twenty-first-century Christians. This psalm condemns our divided allegiances and the lack of wholeness and integration in our lives.

Solomon is saying that if you leave God out of your life and out of your family's life, it is useless to work hard to provide for the material needs of your family. You might work eighty hours a week so you can afford a huge mansion, the best food, the finest clothing, and the most prestigious schools for your children—and it would all be for nothing if you failed to make God the foundation of your family life.

If you leave God out of your family's life, all the material blessings you provide will ruin your children's lives. Instead of being grateful to God for His provision, they'll grow up feeling arrogant and entitled. If God is not the center of your family life, the inheritance you leave your children will be a curse, not a blessing. "In vain you rise early and stay up late, toiling for food to eat," Solomon says, "for he grants sleep to those he loves."

The Old Testament was not written for a Western mindset but an Eastern mindset. The Western mindset divides life into distinct categories. Westerners place "family" in a different category from "work." We maintain separate categories in every aspect of our lives. We separate the spiritual from the temporal, the home from the workplace, Sunday from the other weekdays—and we behave like different people when we are in these other environments.

People who meet us only in the workplace might not recognize us if they saw us at home. People who meet us only at church might not recognize the way we behave at the office. People who know our weekday selves might not recognize our Sunday selves, and vice versa.

But the Bible tells us that those who fear God, love God, and serve God must live an integrated life. The word *integrated* means with all parts seamlessly conjoined and coordinated. It comes from the same Latin root word as *integrity*—the Latin word *integer*, meaning whole. If we have integrity, if our lives are fully integrated, then we are whole—there are no compartments in our lives. All aspects of our lives fit together perfectly and seamlessly.

God at the Center

An old African proverb says that it takes a village to raise a child. The modern-day "village" in this proverb is all society, including schools, houses of worship, doctors, and businesses, but most of all, government programs. Some have used this idea to advocate for various laws, regulations, welfare state programs, and taxpayer support of "family planning" organizations (i.e., Planned Parenthood).

I submit that it does *not* take a village to raise a child. God already designed the perfect nurturing environment for a child. It's called a family. It is pointless to talk about caring for the needs of children while we do nothing to strengthen the family. Children don't need all this meddling by the "village." Children need the family. We need to teach parents how to be parents and how to build healthy families. That means we need to teach moms and dads how to put God at the center of their families.

The "village" that surrounds our families today is a godless village. Prayer has been banned from schools, so the schools cannot help families put God at the center. Welfare state programs cannot help families put God at the center. Planned Parenthood is certainly not going to help families put God at the center. Doctors and businesses are not equipped to help families put God at the center. So the "village" is essentially godless and useless. A godless village can only produce godless children.

From where do godly children come? Only one place: godly families.

The psalmist tells us that unless God is at the center of the family, the family is adrift. Unless God is at the center of our family life, our children will be unsafe, insecure, and in danger. But when we place God at the center of our family, we will see four wonderful results.

Result Number 1: When God is at the center of the family, He will grow the family.

When God builds the house, when God is at the center of the home, the family will grow in faith, character, and maturity. When God's Word fills a home with His wisdom, the insignia of spiritual maturity is imprinted on the souls of each family member. When God's presence permeates the family, there is harmony and peace throughout the household. When the family seeks the mind of God in every important decision, that home becomes a testament to God's grace.

My family could tell you that I have my share of flaws, and I make my fair share of mistakes. I don't say that to appear humble. I am deeply flawed as a Christian, as a husband, and as a father. But as God knows my heart, I can tell you that I honestly seek to put Jesus Christ at the center of our home. His grace has overruled so many of my mistakes. His forgiveness has compensated for my times of impatience and overreaction. His wisdom has corrected my moments of foolishness. I can honestly say that it would have been impossible for my family to grow to a place of Christian maturity if my wife and I had not been daily on our knees, pleading with God on behalf of our family.

It is impossible to raise a family for Christ in this corrosive and anti-Christian culture without hours and hours of prayer. It is impossible to raise a family for Christ in our own flawed and sinful flesh. Only complete reliance on God can enable us to raise our children in the fear and nurture of the Lord.

Result Number 2: When God is at the center of the family, He will bless the family.

Across our culture, families are disintegrating. Children are neglected. Parents are raising their children out of guilt, not love. They give them everything in the world except the most important thing of all—time spent together in prayer and the Word of God.

A well-known Christian leader once told me that before he became a Christian, he viewed his family as a nuisance. They took up his time and got in the way of his ambition for success. He didn't enjoy playing with his kids, talking with his kids, or spending time with his kids. He couldn't wait to leave town on a business trip because all he cared about was worldly success. Once he became a Christian, his priorities changed. Suddenly, he wanted to spend time with his kids, talking with them about Jesus and how God had blessed their family, memorizing Scripture with them, praying with them, playing with them, listening to them.

Once this man put God at the center of his life and his family, God blessed his family and blessed his life. Most importantly, this man began to see his children as a blessing and an inheritance from the Lord.

Solomon is saying to us today that children who are blessed—and children who are a blessing—are brought up to know the Lord. Only when we raise children to love God, to honor their father and mother, and to obey God's Word are they blessed to be a blessing to others.

Result Number 3: When God is at the center of the family, He will guide the family.

Children who observe their parents regularly studying the Word of God for the direction in their lives will grow up seeking guidance from the Word. The habit of seeking direction from the Word is usually caught, not taught. As parents, we impart this habit more by setting an example than by preaching to our children.

How do we find guidance from God's Word? Well, some read God's Word as if it were a fortune cookie. They close their eyes, poke their finger at a random page of the Bible, then read what is written.

I once heard about a man who tried this method of seeking guidance from the Bible. He closed his eyes, poked his finger at a verse, and opened his eyes to read Matthew 27:5, which says, "...he went away and hanged himself." Well, that wasn't what he wanted to hear! He tried again, and this time he chanced upon Luke 10:37, where he read, "Go and do likewise." That was worse! So he tried again and read these words from John 13:27: "What you are about to do, do quickly."

We cannot know the mind of God by randomly selecting bits and pieces of His Word. To find guidance for our daily lives, we need to be daily, regularly, habitually feeding on the Word of God. We need to systematically build God's wisdom into our lives so that when a crisis comes, when it's time to make a difficult decision, we will already have God's answer waiting for us in our hearts.

One of the ways we become wiser, more godly parents is by studying the way God, our heavenly Father, parents us. One of the most profound experiences of Christian parenthood is learning to appreciate God's fatherly love for us. As we go through various joys and trials with our children, we realize again and again, "Oh, *that's* how God rejoices with me, *that's* how God is patient with me, *that's* how God is loving and forgiving with me!"

How can we become the best parents we can be? It's simple. All we have to do is copy the model of God the Father. Study the Fatherhood of God, then do as He does. The story of God's parenting of Israel in the Old Testament and His parenting of the church in the New Testament is the best parenting class you could ever take. Here are some examples.

- In Genesis 28:15, God says, "I am with you and will watch over you wherever you go....I will not leave you." A godly parent is always available, protective, and involved in the child's life.

- In Deuteronomy 20:4, we read, "For the Lord your God is the one who goes with you to fight for you against your enemies to give you victory." A godly parent is always rooting for the child and giving leadership to the child so that he or she can live victoriously.

- In Psalm 149:4, God says, "For the Lord takes delight in his people." A godly parent enjoys being with the child and takes delight in the child. A godly parent lifts up the child and never tears down the child.

- In Jeremiah 31:34, God says, "For I will forgive their wickedness and will remember their sins no more." A godly parent forgives and forgets. A godly parent does not bring up past sins against the child but forgives as if it never happened.

- In Psalm 34:15, God says, "The eyes of the LORD are on the righteous, and his ears are attentive to their cry." God listens to us. He doesn't merely pretend to listen as human parents all too often do. He is attentive to our prayers, our pleadings, and our cries. Godly parents are good listeners. Are we as attentive to our children as God is to us?

- In 1 John 3:1, we read, "See what great love the Father has lavished on us, that we should be called children of God!" Godly parents lavish love on their children. They are quick to tell their children, "I am so proud of you! I love you so much!"

As we grow in our understanding of God's parenting of us, we gain parenting wisdom directly from God. We will never achieve God-like perfection as parents, but we will have the best guidance a parent could have. Our children will still have problems and issues; they may question our teaching for a time as they seek their own identity. But they will grow up to love the Lord because we have modeled God's love to them.

Result Number 4: When God is at the center of the family, He will protect the family.

We live in a dangerous world with bullying and violence in schools, mind-altering drugs in the streets, and predators on the internet and in our neighborhoods. Real dangers are facing our kids and surrounding our families. That's why the psalmist said, "Unless the LORD watches over the city, the guards stand watch in vain" (Ps. 127:1). Let's put those words in today's terms: "Unless God is the protector and defender of our families and communities, the police and first responders can do little to save us."

I thank God for police officers and firefighters and emergency medical workers and the military—all the brave protectors of our families and communities. Now and then, we see an officer killed in the line of duty—and I'm not ashamed to say that I weep when I see such stories in the news. I think of the terrible grief and sadness when a family learns that Dad or Mom won't be coming home from pursuing a suspect or fighting a fire.

But I want to tell you that we have an even greater Guardian than the police or the fire department. That Guardian's name is Jesus. He sends His angels to minister to our families. Unless He is watching over us, all other guardians are in vain.

The psalmist says it is in vain for the guards to watch over the city unless God Himself guards it. The Lord will protect those who place God at the center of their families. Those who place God at the center of their families will find shelter under His wings. Those who place God at the center of their families are engraved on the palms of His hand. You have His word on it.

When God is at the center, God grows the family, God blesses the family, God guides the family, and God protects the family. To revitalize your family, place God at the center of your life, your marriage, and your family.

4

REESTABLISH THE CLASSROOM

I N 2014, A Brawley, California, high school senior named Brooks Hamby turned in his salutatorian speech for approval by the school administrators. The address opened with a brief prayer: "Heavenly Father, in all times, let us always be kind to one another, tenderhearted, forgiving one another, as God in Christ has forgiven us." School officials rejected Hamby's speech, telling him there could be no reference to God.

He rewrote the speech several times, and school officials rejected each version. They marked up one draft with a thick black marker, obliterating all mention of God, warning Brooks that his microphone would be cut off if he uttered one religious word.

Hamby had every right under the First Amendment to speak about his faith in his speech. The First Amendment begins: "Congress shall make no law respecting an establishment of religion, or prohibiting the free exercise thereof; or abridging the freedom of speech...." School officials were violating his constitutional rights.

Determined to obey his conscience and his Lord, Hamby delivered his speech on graduation night, including the prayer. He testified to his faith in Christ. He was amazed that he got through his speech without someone turning off his microphone. Mission accomplished.[1]

In Memphis, Tennessee, an elementary school teacher gave her students an assignment: Tell us about your hero. Ten-year-old Erin Shead's hero was God. She wrote an essay about God's admirable qualities. When she turned it in, her horrified teacher made her leave the classroom and take her paper off school property before anyone else saw it.

Some of the students overheard Erin's teacher admonishing her for writing about God. They gathered around her after class and mocked her for her faith. At home, Erin asked her mother why it's wrong to talk about God in school.[2]

The Free Exercise of Your Child's Faith

The Founding Fathers wrote the First Amendment to protect the very rights that are being suppressed by public schools across America. The First Amendment guarantees a student's right to express his or her religious beliefs, openly and in front of other students, to voluntarily pray and read the Bible on school grounds, and to wear religious symbols, such as a cross.

Unfortunately school administrators and teachers have been bombarded by propaganda from radical anti-Christian organizations like the Freedom From Religion Foundation and the American Civil Liberties Union. As a result, the same First Amendment that was written to defend us from such abuses is used to deny our children their freedom of religion and speech.

The suppression of our children's First Amendment

rights began with a 1962 US Supreme Court case, Engel v. Vitale. The lawsuit was filed by people opposed to a short prayer written for public schools by the New York Board of Regents. The simple twenty-three-word prayer reads: "Almighty God, we acknowledge our dependence upon Thee, and we beg Thy blessings upon us, our parents, our teachers, and our country. Amen." The anti-prayer plaintiffs lost in three lower state courts, including the New York Supreme Court.[3]

But a six-to-one majority of the United States Supreme Court threw a commonsense understanding of the First Amendment out the window. The High Court ruled that by addressing a prayer to "Almighty God," that twenty-three-word prayer constituted the establishment of a state religion. Associate Justice Hugo Black wrote the decision.

> The Founding Fathers wrote the First Amendment to protect the very rights that are being suppressed by public schools across America.

Justice Black was a leftist nominated to the Court by Franklin Delano Roosevelt. Prior to World War II, Black was an outspoken supporter of FDR's failed plan to expand the Supreme Court, pack it with New Deal progressives, and vastly increase FDR's executive powers. During World War II, Black wrote the majority opinion in Korematsu v. the United States, which approved internment camps for Japanese Americans. Before serving on the High Court, Black was a member of the Ku Klux Klan and had delivered many virulently anti-Catholic speeches at Klan rallies. Though Hugo Black resigned from the KKK in 1925, he was granted life membership in the Klan in 1926.[4]

In his written opinion in Engel v. Vitale, Justice Black cited no legal precedents or previous court decisions. He couldn't. In the entire history of the United States Constitution and Bill of Rights, no court had ever banned any prayer of any kind for any reason. The High Court decision was simply unprecedented.

Justice Potter Stewart dissented, noting that the government had frequently endorsed prayers and religious observances without establishing a state religion. He pointed out that the Supreme Court itself opens with the declaration, "God save the United States and this Honorable Court," which is a prayerful invocation. The Senate and House of Representatives open each session with prayer. Every president since George Washington has taken the oath of office, asking for protection and guidance from God.

Yet *schoolchildren* were forbidden to acknowledge God at the beginning of their school day? This glaring contradiction exposed the hypocrisy of the Court's opinion.

Educating a Menace to Society

The First Amendment contains two clauses regarding religion, the Establishment Clause ("Congress shall make no law respecting an establishment of religion") and the Free Exercise Clause ("or prohibiting the free exercise thereof"). Justice Stewart argued persuasively that the New York Regents' prayer did not violate the Establishment Clause. In fact, banning the prayer would clearly violate the Free Exercise Clause. Unfortunately Stewart's reasoning did not prevail.

We tend to view the Supreme Court as the ultimate word on all matters involving the Constitution. We easily forget how many times the Supreme Court has gotten it wrong. One of the worst Supreme Court decisions of all time was the infamous Dred Scott decision of March 6, 1857. Chief Justice Roger Taney, a racist Southern aristocrat, wrote the opinion, which stated that all people of African descent—whether free or slave—were not United States citizens and that all slaves were property, not people. The American Civil War was one of the disastrous consequences of that decision—and many destructive effects of that decision continue to this day.

Like the Dred Scott decision, the decision in Engel v. Vitale was an attempt to settle a contentious social question with a ruling that went far beyond the language of the Constitution. The Establishment Clause was intended to prevent America from establishing a state religion like the Church of England. A twenty-three-word nonsectarian prayer at the beginning of the school day does not establish a state religion.

As Christians we must not accept a state decree banning God from the public schools. Graduating high schoolers have a First Amendment right to declare their faith in commencement speeches. Elementary school students have a First Amendment right to witness to their friends, to read their Bible, and to write about their love for God in class assignments.

By banning God from the classroom, we have invited a rise in school violence, drug abuse, bullying, depression, and suicide. As Theodore Roosevelt once observed,

"To educate a man in the mind and not in morals is to educate a menace to society."[5] Our schools no longer teach young people how to think for themselves, how to reason, how to live moral and productive lives, or how to recognize propaganda and logical fallacies. Instead, our schools have become godless indoctrination centers.

Let's not blame the teachers. The vast majority of public school teachers I've met are dedicated professionals who genuinely love their students. I've spoken with many teachers who feel trapped by an inflexible system that prevents them from doing the job they wish they could do. Hamstrung by the demands of the "politically correct" federal and state education establishments, and undermined by apathetic parents, these teachers are doing their best under impossible conditions. We urgently need to reestablish a strong, values-centered, faith-respecting education system.

Controlling Your Child's Mind

If you are a parent of school-age children, you've undoubtedly heard of Common Core. The Common Core State Standards Initiative is a federal program that defines what kindergarten-through-twelfth-grade students in the United States should know in math and English. It was developed with funding by the Bill & Melinda Gates Foundation and implemented by the Obama administration and the National Governors Association.

One formative influence on Common Core was Bill Ayers, the radical leader of the 1960s domestic terror group the Weather Underground. From 1970 to 1972, Ayers took part in the bombings of New York City police headquarters, the Capitol building, and the Pentagon. He is said to have summed up the Weather Underground slogan as, "Kill all the rich people.... Bring the revolution home. Kill your parents." By the 1980s, an unrepentant Bill Ayers had reinvented himself as a professor of education at the University of Illinois.[6]

In October 2009, an elite education consortium, the Renaissance Group, held a three-day conference in Washington, DC. The conference introduced the "Common Core State Standards" initiative. Three keynote addresses were delivered, two by Obama officials, Secretary of Education Arne Duncan and Under Secretary of Education Martha Kanter, and one by Bill Ayers.

Ayers' role in shaping Common Core standards is shrouded in secrecy. As the Horowitz Freedom Center explains, "What Ayers spoke about at this conference was never publicly revealed, but his participation as a keynoter clearly indicates that his opinions were given considerable weight."[7]

Common Core was introduced in 2010 with a four-billion-dollar pot of federal grant money to entice state governments into the program. Forty-six of the fifty states jumped aboard. Only Alaska, Nebraska, Texas, and Virginia rejected this radical experiment. As of 2020, four states have withdrawn from Common Core—Arizona, Indiana, Oklahoma, and South Carolina. At least twelve more states have begun repealing Common Core.[8]

After initially embracing Common Core, Indiana made an abrupt U-turn away from this massive educational gamble. The credit for Indiana's turnabout goes to two Indianapolis moms, Heather Crossin and Erin Tuttle.

In September 2011, after Common Core was implemented in Indiana, Heather Crossin noticed a change in her eight-year-old daughter's math homework. As Crossin told an interviewer, "Instead of many arithmetic problems, the homework would contain only three or four questions, and two of those would be 'explain your answer.' Like, 'One bridge is 412 feet long and the other bridge is 206 feet long. Which bridge is longer? How do you know?'"[9]

Crossin had always been able to help her daughter with her homework. Now she was at a loss. Answering the "how do you know" question required knowledge of Common Core jargon—and Heather Crossin was an outsider to the lingo. It was as if Common Core was teaching children a secret language, making it impossible for parents to help their third-grade children with their arithmetic.

Significantly, Heather Crossin's daughter attended a private Catholic school, not a public school. Crossin soon learned that other parents were complaining about the new math program. The school held a meeting and brought in a saleswoman from the textbook company to smooth over the parents' concerns. The saleswoman, Crossin recalled, "told us we were all so very, very lucky, because our children were using one of the very first Common Core-aligned textbooks in the country."[10]

Crossin didn't feel "lucky." She learned that public schools had adopted this radical approach to math. Their Catholic school had fallen in line with Common Core because the new Indiana assessment tests required all students, including private school students, to meet

Common Core standards. More than half of Catholic dioceses nationwide have adopted Common Core.[11]

Before that meeting, Heather Crossin hadn't heard of Common Core. She contacted local journalists and found they'd never heard of it either. Crossin contacted a state legislator on the Indiana senate's Education Committee, and even he knew nothing about Indiana's adoption of Common Core. She searched online for news coverage about the state Board of Education's decision to adopt Common Core. No coverage. The Board of Education had made a sweeping decision without notifying legislators, media, parents, or taxpayers.

At around the same time, Heather Crossin's friend Erin Tuttle noticed a change in her child's English homework. Instead of assigning great literature to read, the Catholic school English program now assigned *Time* magazine's *Time For Kids* simplified "informational texts," many of which had a secular-left slant.

The more she looked into the English standards for Common Core, the clearer it became that Common Core was being promoted by education elites, profit-making textbook publishers, and nationwide testing companies. Common Core was not teaching kids how to enrich their lives through great literature. It was dispensing "politically correct" messages through *Time For Kids*.

After discovering the harm Common Core was causing in their Catholic school, Heather Crossin and Erin Tuttle went on an eighteen-month odyssey to restore traditional education to Indiana. They reached out to traditional values organizations such as the Hoover Institution, the Heritage Foundation, the Pioneer Institute, the

American Principles Project, Americans for Prosperity, and the Indiana Association of Home Educators. They traveled up and down the state, speaking at rallies and town halls and giving countless media interviews. Their efforts resulted in Indiana's repeal of Common Core, signed by then-governor Mike Pence. Indiana's repeal triggered a wave of repeal efforts in other states, many of them successful, others still ongoing.

These two Indiana moms set an example for us all, proving that Americans can raise their voices to defeat a well-funded education/indoctrination establishment.

The Theory That Failed

The *stated* goal of Common Core was to bring American students' test scores up to the levels of other high-achieving nations such as Japan, Estonia, Canada, Finland, and South Korea. But if that was the goal of Common Core, why were Common Core standards so radically unlike the standards in those countries? While the top-scoring students in the world were learning math using traditional teaching methods, American students were used as guinea pigs in a nationwide experiment, subjecting their developing minds to a completely untried, untested curriculum.

The designers of Common Core set up a panel of education experts called the Common Core State Standards Validation Committee—then proceeded to ignore the experts' recommendations. One member of the Validation Committee, Sandra Stotsky, a nationally recognized authority on education standards, said, "The real role of this committee [was] more like that of a rubber stamp." After their critiques were repeatedly disregarded, Stotsky concluded, "I, along with four other members of the Validation Committee, declined to sign off on the final version."[12]

Another member of the Common Core State Standards Validation Committee is Stanford University mathematics professor R. James Milgram. He told the Texas state legislature that the Common Core agenda "does not adequately reflect our current understanding of why the math programs in the high-achieving countries give dramatically better results."[13]

Milgram also spoke before the Indiana Senate Education Committee and said, "The Common Core standards claim to be 'benchmarked against international standards' but this phrase is meaningless. They are actually two or more years behind international expectations by eighth grade, and only fall further behind" in later grades.[14]

Let's speak plainly: The Common Core promoters' claims that the program would bring American students up to international standards were designed to fool us into thinking that Common Core's *downgraded* standards are really an upgrade. In part because of the testimony of Stotsky and Milgram, Texas never adopted Common Core.[15]

Common Core standards are not based on evidence, but secular-left social engineering theory. Less than a decade after the inception of Common Core, the theory was utterly disproven. As of 2018, student scores on the ACT (the American College Testing admissions exam) had fallen to a twenty-year low. Student preparedness for college-level English was at its worst level since 2002; preparedness for college-level math was the worst since 2004.[16]

The American education system has traditionally been designed to give parents, teachers, lawmakers, and community officials local control over education. But in state after state, the public was kept in the dark about the content, standards, and costs of implementing Common Core—until it was too late. Common Core standards and curricula are owned and copyrighted by two private trade organizations that are unaccountable to educators and parents.

The more closely you examine Common Core, the more it appears that the goal of the program was *not* to prepare students for college, and *not* to enable American students to compete with students in other nations. Instead, Common Core seems intended to *dumb down* educational standards. Why would anyone want to do that to America's schoolchildren?

It may be because Common Core was designed *not* by educators, but by policymakers and social engineers whose goal is *indoctrination*. Does that sound like a wacky conspiracy theory? Well, listen to what Common Core leaders are saying.

Our Children as Guinea Pigs

One of the keynote speakers at the Common Core Standards Institute conference in July 2018 was Kate Gerson, CEO of UnboundEd, an organization with enormous influence over Common Core implementation across America. Through its Common Core Standards Institute, UnboundEd trains thousands of teachers. Gerson makes several shocking statements in her talk, including this [emphasis added]:

> We stigmatize our students, we look at our students in a way that expects less of them when they are not white. This is a phenomenon that is real. It is happening all the time. You cannot be cured from it. White people in particular, I want to say this to you: *if you are under the impression that there are good white people and bad white people, you are wrong.* And you must open yourself to be confronted with more and more and more information about the ways in which your beliefs, to which you don't necessarily have access, and your behavior, which you don't necessarily see, is informing your work, day in and day out.[17]

That statement comes from "The Intersection of Standards and Equity," a video posted online by UnboundEd. You can view it at YouTube.com and see how our teachers are being indoctrinated so that they can indoctrinate your child. Gerson is saying that every teacher of European ancestry is a racist. This statement dehumanizes and stigmatizes every individual within an entire ethnic identity. And dehumanizing and stigmatizing people because of the color of their skin is the essence of bigotry.

One of the worst labels to place on a person is *racist*. That label can cost you your career, your reputation, and your ability to earn a living. Yet terms like *racist* and *white supremacist* have been dangerously weaponized in our society. Kevin Drum, a writer for the far-left magazine *Mother Jones*, warns his fellow leftists that these terms have become so overused that they have lost all meaning.

> With the exception of actual neo-Nazis and a few others, there isn't anyone in America who's trying to promote the idea that whites are inherently superior to blacks or Latinos....It's bad enough that liberals toss around charges of racism with more abandon than we should, but it's far worse if we start calling every sign of racial animus—big or small, accidental or deliberate—white supremacy. I can hardly imagine a better way of proving to the non-liberal community that we're all a bunch of out-of-touch nutbars who are going to label everyone and everything we don't like as racist.[18]

It's good to encourage teachers to believe in their students, regardless of race and ethnicity. We should challenge all students to reach for their potential. But does Common Core have to stigmatize all teachers of one ethnicity to achieve that goal?

Kate Gerson's UnboundEd is a spin-off of EngageNY. This organization works with the New York State Department of Education to develop Common Core–compliant curricula for New York public schools. Gerson sees UnboundEd as a company that produces resources for teachers that wrap around EngageNY's curricula. "We knew that the curriculum would change the game," Gerson said.[19]

EngageNY has an enormous influence on Common Core schools nationwide, offering an online repository of free resources for teachers. According to a 2017 report by the Rand Corporation, EngageNY's Common Core resources had attracted more than seventeen million users nationwide, generating more than sixty-six million downloads. Rand found that nearly a third of math teachers and more than a quarter of English language arts teachers across America use EngageNY's Common Core materials.[20] So this one New York–based organization, EngageNY, is having an astounding impact on what teachers across America are teaching our kids.

The progressive education reformers have decided that the great challenge facing American education today is teachers with racist attitudes. Out of this misguided notion, they are conducting this nationwide experiment with our children as guinea pigs.

Who Is a Terrorist?

As a Christian boy growing up in Egypt under Islamic and socialist tyranny, I longed for freedom. As a young man, I went to libraries and checked out books on American history and ideals. I was fascinated and amazed by the freedoms Americans enjoyed. I learned about the founding of the United States—and one of the stories that inspired me as a boy was this one.

On the night of December 16, 1773, three British ships were docked in Boston harbor, laden with tea. That night a group of patriots known as the Sons of Liberty boarded the boats. For three hours, they opened containers and dumped the entire cargo of tea in the harbor.

This was not an unruly mob. They didn't riot, loot, or vandalize the ships, and they didn't harm or terrorize anyone. They were careful not to destroy anything but tea. In fact, when one of the men accidentally broke a padlock, the group immediately sent ashore for a replacement padlock. The Sons of Liberty wanted their protest against oppressive taxation to be dignified and nonviolent.

This act of protest became known as the Boston Tea Party. It was masterminded by a devoutly Christian Puritan named Samuel Adams. His cousin, future US president John Adams, later wrote in his diary that the Boston Tea Party was "the most magnificent movement of all. There is a dignity, a majesty, a sublimity in this last effort of the patriots that I greatly admire."[21]

Why am I sharing this story? I tell it because American schoolchildren have been told that the Boston Tea Party participants were "terrorists." A terrorist, by definition, uses murder and intimidation against innocent civilians to achieve political goals. The Boston Tea Partiers were scrupulously nonviolent and didn't terrorize anyone. Calling them "terrorists" is not only dishonest but absurd. What a tragedy that these freedom-loving patriots should be compared to the bloodthirsty likes of Osama bin Laden.

This false characterization of the Boston Tea Party was concocted by CSCOPE, a program of the Texas Education Service Centers of the Texas public schools.[22] Lying about the Boston Tea Party is bad enough—but it gets worse. CSCOPE not only smeared early American patriots as terrorists, but it also whitewashed *real* al Qaeda terrorists as "freedom fighters." CSCOPE's depiction of terrorists as freedom fighters came to light as a result of a unit on Islam taught in ninth-grade geography classes in Texas.

In the Lumberton, Texas, school district, a ninth-grade

geography teacher brought in burqas (fundamentalist Islamic garb for women) and asked some of the girls to dress up and have their pictures taken. One volunteer was Madelyn LeBlanc, age fifteen. After the photo was posted to social media, the administration called Madelyn and the other girls in to sign an "incident report," stating in writing they had not been coerced into wearing the burqas.

Madelyn knew something wasn't right. She called her mother and told her that the school had made her sign a statement. In minutes Mrs. LeBlanc was in the school office demanding to know what her daughter had signed.

The CSCOPE curriculum had presented the burqa as a harmless feature of a foreign culture, when, in fact, the burqa is a sign of the oppression and subjugation of women by fundamentalist Islam. Madelyn's mother told a local news channel that her daughter "didn't really know the history of a burqa. I think she regrets doing it now, because she learned about the oppression behind it."

Texas Board of Education member David Bradley expressed his dismay that the Islamic curriculum was imposed by CSCOPE "without any oversight, without any accountability, and we've started to discover things like a lack of emphasis of patriotism" alongside an "encouragement in the virtues of communism."[23]

Though Texas had officially rejected Common Core standards, the radicals within the Texas education establishment have continued to indoctrinate Texas schoolchildren into an anti-American values system. The progressives have a monopoly on textbooks, curriculum, and teacher's resources. That is how they control the agenda for our schools.

People who portray freedom fighters as terrorists and terrorists as freedom fighters should not be allowed within a thousand miles of our children's education. As the Old Testament warns, "Woe to those who call evil good and good evil, who put darkness for light and light for darkness, who put bitter for sweet and sweet for bitter" (Isa. 5:20).

The Assault on Homeschoolers

Most teachers are dedicated, caring professionals committed to their students' growth and learning. Many feel trapped by an inflexible, bureaucratic system that prevents them from giving their students a quality learning environment. These teachers do the best they can despite the government-imposed curriculum they must teach—a curriculum that often violates the faith and moral values of Christian families.

Many parents are fighting back against the exclusion of God from public education in the only way they can: they educate their children at home.

Homeschool parents make enormous sacrifices to educate their children. Their reasons for homeschooling include (1) making sure their children receive a high-quality education; (2) preventing their children from being indoctrinated by false values; and (3) providing the spiritual and moral instruction that public schools don't offer.

The coronavirus (COVID-19) crisis of early 2020 hugely impacted both public schools and the homeschool community. Across America, public schools closed, and schoolchildren "attended class" via the internet. Suddenly parents could see what their schoolchildren were being taught—and some parents were shocked to discover how much time was spent on indoctrination instead of instruction.

An April 2020 RealClear Opinion Research poll of registered voters revealed a surprising finding: 40.8 percent of families reported they were more likely to abandon public schools in favor of schooling at home once the coronavirus restrictions ended. Additionally, 64 percent reported favoring school choice measures such as education vouchers. You might think the polling sample was skewed toward Republicans (who traditionally favor homeschooling more than Democrats do), but survey participants were 45.7 percent Democrat and 42.3 percent Republican.[24]

> People who portray freedom fighters as terrorists and terrorists as freedom fighters should not be allowed within a thousand miles of our children's education.

The shutdown of the public school system during the coronavirus pandemic has given parents time to reflect on the best options for educating their children. Many are strongly considering teaching kids at home.

Yet homeschooling families are under assault from public school officials, secular-left legislators, and teachers' unions. In February 2008, a California court ruled against approximately 166,000 homeschooled children in the state, establishing a requirement that homeschool parents must have valid teaching credentials. Parents without credentials would have to send their children to public school or face fines and imprisonment. The decision was, for all practical purposes, a ban on homeschooling.

The powerful California Teachers Association applauded the ruling. Forcing 166,000 children into public schools would mean more teacher hiring and more union dues. "We're happy," said Lloyd Porter of the CTA. "We always think students should be taught by credentialed teachers, no matter what the setting."[25]

Fortunately the California court ruling did not stand. Six months later, the Court of Appeal for the Second Appellate District in California overturned the earlier decision. Homeschoolers were free to continue their education at home.[26] But the war was not over. The attacks on homeschooling continued.

In July 2016, weeks before public school student registration was to begin, the San Benito High School District sent a letter to homeschool parents stating that "under California Law, a home school is not a private school, nor is it a lawful alternative to public school."[27] Was it a ploy to frighten parents into registering their children at public school? Or were the school officials ignorant of the appellate court's ruling in 2008? We only know that the school district quietly dropped the matter without explanation.

In 2018, California lawmakers made another move to limit homeschooling, this time through Assembly Bill 2756. Authored by Democrat Assemblyman José Medina, AB 2756 would have required all homeschool families in California to submit to involuntary home inspections.

Word of the pending legislation brought hundreds of homeschool families to Sacramento in April for a late-night session of the Assembly Education Committee. After hearing from homeschool parents, the committee voted the bill down.[28]

We see the real agenda of homeschool opponents in this statement by atheist attorney (and former editor of *The Nation*) Paul Blanshard: "I think that the most important factor moving us toward a secular society has been the educational factor. Our schools may not teach Johnny to read properly, but the fact that Johnny is in school until he is sixteen tends to lead toward the elimination of religious superstition."[29] Homeschoolers teach the biblical beliefs and godly values that Blanshard condemns as "superstition."

If the opponents of homeschooling truly cared about quality education for kids, they'd be the biggest *supporters* of homeschooling. Homeschooled students consistently perform better than public school students on standardized tests. A nationwide study commissioned by the Home School Legal Defense Association and conducted by Dr. Brian D. Ray of the National Home Education Research Institute examined 11,739 students from all fifty states, Guam, and Puerto Rico. The study concluded:

> Homeschoolers are still achieving well beyond their public school counterparts—no matter what their family background, socioeconomic level, or style of homeschooling.
>
> In the study, homeschoolers scored 34–39 percentile points higher than the norm on

standardized achievement tests. The homeschool national average ranged from the 84th percentile for Language, Math, and Social Studies to the 89th percentile for Reading.

The study also found that whether or not parents were teacher-certified had no impact on these high scores. Critics of homeschooling have long insisted that parents who want to teach their own children should become certified teachers first. But in this study, students received slightly higher scores if neither parent had ever held a state-issued teaching certificate than if one or both parents had. Critics also insist that the government should regulate homeschooling in order to ensure the quality of education that students receive. However, in this study, the degree to which homeschooling was regulated by state governments had no bearing on student test scores.[30]

The reasons may have a lot to do with the highly individualized attention homeschooled kids receive. When a teacher has only a few students instead of thirty, those few students are bound to excel.

The May–June 2020 issue of *Harvard Magazine* featured an interview with Elizabeth Bartholet, faculty director of Harvard Law School's Child Advocacy Program and a persistent critic of homeschooling. The magazine said that Bartholet recommends "a presumptive ban" on homeschooling because the practice "violates children's right to a 'meaningful education'" as well as their "right to be protected from potential child abuse."

Bartholet's stated rationale for "a presumptive ban" on

homeschooling is the secular-left myth that large numbers of homeschool parents are child abusers. In her view, homeschooling gives abusive parents a convenient dodge to keep kids out of school. She wants parents to be forced to send their children to government schools where teachers must report any suspicion of abuse to Child Protective Services.

Hundreds of thousands of children are educated at home every year, and they are thriving and outperforming their public schooled peers. What's more, they are not subjected to bullying, schoolyard violence, secularist indoctrination, and attacks on their faith and moral values. Homeschool parents take on the added responsibility of teaching their children, even while paying taxes to support the public schools—*not* because they are abusive parents, but because they are *loving* parents.

Elizabeth Bartholet is a social engineer who thinks the government knows better than parents what is best for a child. She views parents as dangerous authoritarians who threaten the well-being of children. She asks, "Do we think that parents should have 24/7, essentially authoritarian control over their children from ages zero to 18? I think that's dangerous. I think it's always dangerous to put powerful people in charge of the powerless, and to give the powerful ones total authority."[31]

Bartholet is oblivious to the irony of her own words. Yes, it's dangerous to put powerful people in total authority over our children—but the powerful people I fear most are not parents, but progressive social engineers.

The Screwtape Proposal

Homeschooling is not an option for all parents. While I defend Christian homeschooling, I also support and applaud teachers and families in the public school system. Whether our kids are in homeschool or public school, they face challenges and need our prayers and support.

Parents, be aware of the forces at school that seek to reshape the beliefs of your children. Stay attuned to what your children are being taught. Ask them questions about their day and what they are learning (dinnertime is an excellent time for these conversations).

> **While I defend Christian homeschooling, I also support and applaud teachers and families in the public school system.**

If you hear anything that troubles you, don't jump to conclusions. Gather all the facts before taking action. Be as supportive as you can of public school teachers. They are often caught in a crossfire between what they must teach and the ire of offended parents.

Empower your children to be bold Christian witnesses at school. Pray with them and help them memorize Scripture. Encourage them to speak openly about their faith. Every day, when you send your children to school, ask for God's protection over them. Go into your children's bedrooms at night and pray over them as they sleep. Ask God to armor-plate your children against the attacks of Satan and this fallen world.

In "Screwtape Proposes a Toast," a 1959 sequel to *The Screwtape Letters* (1942), C. S. Lewis predicted the state of public education today. He depicts the devil Screwtape plotting to destroy young minds through a corrupted public education system:

> The basic principle of the new education is to be that dunces and idlers must not be made to feel inferior to intelligent and industrious pupils. That would be "undemocratic." These differences between the pupils...must be disguised. This can be done on various levels....At schools, the children who are too stupid or lazy to learn languages and mathematics and elementary science can be set to doing the things that children used to do in their spare time. Let them, for example, make mud-pies and call it modeling....Whatever nonsense they are engaged in must have—I believe the English already use the phrase—"parity of esteem."
>
> Of course this would not follow unless all education became state education. But it will.[32]

That is Screwtape's plan for our children. We are living in Screwtape's world—a world in which nearly all education is state-run education, and the government school system seeks to eradicate all competition, including homeschooling. As Christians, we are at war with Screwtape and his ilk. We are fighting for the souls of a generation—and the fight goes on.

RESPECT OUR FREEDOMS

O N THE AFTERNOON of January 31, 2020, Dr. Anthony Fauci stepped up to the microphone in the James S. Brady Press Briefing Room of the White House. Few Americans had ever heard of Dr. Fauci prior to that day, but he would soon become world-famous as one of the lead members of the President's White House Coronavirus Task Force.

He spoke about an outbreak of a strange new virus called the coronavirus or COVID-19. It was a disease, he said, with "a lot of unknowns" and "the number of cases have steeply inclined each and every day." It could be spread by people who showed no symptoms, who gave every appearance of being perfectly healthy. "We still have a low risk to the American public," he concluded, "but we want to keep it at a low risk."[1]

But as it turned out, the American public was at much greater risk from the coronavirus than Dr. Fauci realized. The White House Coronavirus Task Force press briefings grew more frequent—and more troubling. Dr. Fauci and his colleagues talked about the growing danger the coronavirus posed to the elderly and people with underlying health conditions. We heard how our health care system could be overwhelmed by this global pandemic unless all Americans cooperated to contain the disease. We listened—and we cooperated.

Across the nation, many churches, including The Church of The Apostles in Atlanta, complied with state guidelines, suspended regular worship services, and offered online worship services instead. Our ministry team prayed for the physical and spiritual health of our church, our community, and our nation. We supplied numerous online resources for our church family. Through live-streamed worship services, our members continued to grow closer together in the Lord while sheltering in place at home.

Our church was no different from countless other churches across America, all voluntarily forgoing our First Amendment right to exercise our religion freely and assemble peaceably. We were no different from numerous Americans who had voluntarily closed businesses, postponed elective surgery, kept kids home from school, and on and on. Some people endured heartbreaking losses, standing by helplessly as loved ones died in isolation wards.

James Madison and the other framers of the Constitution didn't envision a global pandemic when they wrote the simple, powerful words of the First Amendment: "Congress shall make no law respecting an establishment of religion, or prohibiting the free exercise thereof; or abridging the freedom of speech, or of the press; or the right of the people peaceably to assemble, and to petition the Government for a redress of grievances."[2]

Those forty-five words guarantee all Americans five precious rights: freedom of religion, speech, the press, peaceful assembly, and petitioning the government. But to save lives during the COVID-19 crisis of early 2020, federal and state governments suspended the First Amendment—and conscientious Americans willingly complied.

A Sickening Virus—Then a Sickening Video

In some states, such as my home state of Georgia, government officials expressed gratitude for the sacrifices we all made to contain the spread of COVID-19. On April 20, Governor Brian Kemp announced a limited and cautious reopening of the state's economy. Governor Kemp expressed his appreciation to the people for their voluntary cooperation. "Thank you," he said. "Your sacrifice saved lives."[3]

With typical journalistic overkill, *The Atlantic* described Governor Kemp's reopening of the state economy as "Georgia's Experiment in Human Sacrifice."[4] CNN's scare headline read, "Georgia's Daily Coronavirus Deaths Will Nearly Double by August With Relaxed Social Distancing, Model Suggests."[5] *The Atlanta Journal and Constitution* fretted about whether Georgia would have enough hospital beds for the coming waves of patients. "The news is generally bleak. Revised projections show that unless people act as if they remain on lockdown, infections and deaths by COVID-19 are bound to rise. The only disagreement among experts is by how much and when."[6]

Did these dire predictions come true? No. Even the avowedly left-leaning Vox.com had to admit that, despite predictions of a "sustained spike" of cases and "a surge in deaths," more than a month after the state reopened, "the total of daily new cases has remained relatively flat."[7]

Then, on May 25, 2020, our already-devastated nation suffered an additional horrifying shock: the on-camera death of George Floyd, a forty-six-year-old African American, killed by a white Minneapolis police officer while under arrest and in handcuffs. The disturbing video showed the officer kneeling on Floyd's neck for nearly nine minutes as Floyd begged for his life, saying, "I can't breathe."

I can't watch that sickening video without tears and physical revulsion. It became a symbol of an alleged pattern of racism and brutality in the American criminal justice system. Local protests in the Minneapolis and Saint Paul area quickly spread nationwide. Protests were mostly peaceful in the daytime, but nightfall often brought out rioters, looters, arsonists, and murderers.[8]

As America burned, some irresponsible journalists threw fuel on the flames. CNN anchor Chris Cuomo (whose brother, Andrew Cuomo, is the current governor of New York) defended the mob violence on his *Cuomo Prime Time* show. "Please," he said, "show me where it says protesters are supposed to be polite and peaceful."[9]

Well, the First Amendment speaks of "the right of the people *peaceably* to assemble, and to petition the Government for a redress of grievances." Note that all-important word *peaceably*. The framers of the Constitution understood that the roar of a rioting mob drowns out the voices of peaceful demonstrators.

In August 2020, as American cities from Seattle to New York were being burned and looted, the Hachette Book Group released *In Defense of Looting* by Vicky

Osterweil, a white, transgendered individual who writes for *The Nation* and Al Jazeera America. The book (which might also be titled *In Defense of Barbarianism* or *How to Destroy Civilization*) was highly touted on National Public Radio (NPR), which receives your tax dollars via the Corporation for Public Broadcasting. Drenched in Marxist dogma, the book features a crowbar on the cover—a weapon that was wielded in the 2020 riots against both windows and human beings. NPR describes Osterweil's argument this way:

> As protests and riots continue to grip cities, she stakes out a provocative position: that looting is a powerful tool to bring about real, lasting change in society. The rioters who smash windows and take items from stores, she claims, are engaging in a powerful tactic that questions the justice of "law and order," and the distribution of property and wealth in an unequal society.[10]

What "real, lasting change in society" does the author promote in *In Defense of Looting*? The kind of "lasting change" the rioters and looters produced in the final days of the Roman Empire? Should we celebrate as our civilization is burned to the ground? In its interview with Osterweil, NPR never challenges the author's ugly ideas, but appears to approve them. For example, NPR never pushes back against this statement by Osterweil:

> [Looting] attacks the idea of property, and it attacks the idea that in order for someone to have a roof over their head or have a meal ticket, they have to work for a boss, in order to buy things that

people just like them somewhere else in the world had to make under the same conditions. It points to the way in which that's unjust. And the reason that the world is organized that way, obviously, is for the profit of the people who own the stores and the factories. So you get to the heart of that property relation, and demonstrate that without police and without state oppression, we can have things for free.[11]

I would like to hear Osterweil make this case to the Lee family, who emigrated from South Korea and invested twenty-five years of their lives to build up a beauty supply business, Uptown Beauty, in Kenosha, Wisconsin. The Lees worked long hours, including holidays, to make a living—then they lost everything when their store was demolished by rioters and looters on August 24, 2020, the day before *In Defense of Looting* was released. I would like to hear Osterweil make that case to the thousands of small business owners who lost everything, and their employees who lost their jobs. Many were hardworking immigrants like the Lees—and many others were African Americans.[12]

I wonder how Vicky Osterweil, her publisher, and NPR would explain the social benefits of looting to the family of David Dorn. He was a retired police captain, a Black husband, father, and grandfather who was murdered execution-style by looters as he protected a St. Louis pawnshop in the early hours of June 2, 2020.[13] How is the destruction of immigrant-run stores and the murder of Black police officers justified by what White slave owners did two or three centuries ago?

In Matthew 5, Jesus pronounces His blessing on the poor in spirit, the sorrowing, the humble, the righteous, the merciful, the pure in heart, and the peacemakers. Jesus blesses the peacemakers, not the rioters and looters. The Old Testament tells us, "Speak up and judge fairly; defend the rights of the poor and needy" (Prov. 31:9), which is what a peaceful protester does. But the Old Testament warns, "Whoever sows injustice reaps calamity, and the rod they wield in fury will be broken" (Prov. 22:8).

So there it is in God's Word: we should be stirred to speak up against violence and injustice. But when we speak, we must speak words of peace. Rioting, looting, and burning are intolerable in any civilized society. Anyone who defends mob violence stands rebuked by the laws of God and humanity.

A Double Standard

There was a disconnect between the way state and local governments responded to the protests versus the way those same governments treated other citizens and groups, including churches. When the protests spread nationwide, the governor of New Jersey said, "I support these protests and I thank the thousands of residents who peacefully and respectfully took part....Peaceful protesting is the way we get to a better place." No argument there. Peaceful protests are an American tradition going back to the Boston Tea Party.

But then the governor went a step too far: "It's one thing to protest what day nail salons are opening and it's another to come out in peaceful protest overwhelmingly about somebody who was murdered right before our eyes."[14]

Just a moment, Governor. Yes, it's a sacred constitutional right of the people to peaceably assemble and petition the government for the redress of grievances—and the unjust death of George Floyd grieves us deeply. But the government should not be so dismissive of the right of the people to earn a living. During the coronavirus emergency, some businesses were deemed "essential," while others were "nonessential." The governor of New Jersey may not think a nail salon is an "essential" business—but to the people who built that business and to the employees who work there, that nail salon is absolutely essential to their lives and their families.

The Declaration of Independence tells us that we are endowed by God with "certain unalienable Rights, that among these are Life, Liberty and the pursuit of Happiness." The right to earn a living is basic to life, liberty, and happiness. During the coronavirus crisis, "We the People" willingly set aside our "unalienable rights," but the government should not take our sacrifice for granted. The governor of New Jersey thanked the protesters, but did he ever thank the citizens and businesses and churches for their sacrifice? No.

Even as the governor praised the protesters, he kept churches closed. In fact, churches wouldn't begin to reopen until *two weeks* after the governor made those remarks—and only on an extremely restricted basis. Church buildings that seated two or three thousand people could have easily accommodated hundreds of worshipers with "social distancing"—yet the New Jersey governor mandated a maximum of fifty worshipers in any church service, regardless of the size of the building. The restrictions were simply arbitrary and unjust.

As the Declaration of Independence reminds us, "to secure these rights, Governments are instituted among Men, deriving their just powers from the consent of the governed."[15] "We the People" expect our leaders to use their authority to respect and defend our rights.

It would have been refreshing to hear governors and health officials in every state say, "We understand the incredible sacrifices you make by closing your businesses and houses of worship. We understand you are voluntarily setting aside your sacred rights and even your livelihoods to lower the death toll of this virus. We promise not to keep your businesses and houses of worship closed one minute longer than is absolutely necessary."

Our leaders need to see themselves as servants, not bosses. They need to graciously *thank* the people for their cooperation—not threaten them if they don't comply. Unfortunately, all too many government officials express condescension toward the people they govern. For example:

- The governor of Michigan talked to her citizens as if she were lecturing naughty children: "This is not a suggestion. These are not thoughts about how you can protect yourself. This is the force of law. And we expect the people to follow the law."[16]

- In California, the governor permitted "cannabis retailers" (marijuana dispensaries) to remain open as "essential" businesses while churches were ordered closed.[17]

- In Dane County, Wisconsin, the government permitted bars, restaurants, gyms, theaters, bowling alleys, and trampoline facilities to reopen at 25 percent of capacity—yet churches were restricted to a fifty-person limit regardless of size. This meant many churches were restricted to less than 5 percent of capacity. The county health department called Catholic churches, informing them that undercover observers would surveil the churches and levy fines of up to $1,000 if more than fifty people attended. County officials relented when the Diocese of Madison threatened to go to court.[18]

When the government suppresses religious gatherings while voicing enthusiasm for street protests, when it considers marijuana "essential" and freedom of religion expendable, there is a dangerous double standard at work.

What Religious Freedom Really Means

When politicians talk about our freedoms, they often use the phrase "freedom of worship" instead of the First Amendment term, "the free exercise of religion." Do the specific words matter? Yes, they do.

"Freedom of worship" means you are free to worship *inside your church* any way you choose. Many politicians, judges, and secular-left activists want you to keep your religion behind church doors, where no one else can see or hear it. They don't want you talking about your faith in the classroom, on campus, or in a public park. They don't want to see you praying or singing Christian songs in front of a government building.

That's why the precise wording of the First Amendment is so important. It guarantees the *free exercise* of religion, not just freedom of worship. We are free to exercise our faith at work, on campus, in the neighborhood, on the military base, and everywhere else. We do not merely have freedom of worship one day a week. We are free to exercise our religion twenty-four hours a day, seven days a week. Two recent Supreme Court cases illustrate the importance of the First Amendment guarantee of the free exercise of religion.

First, there's the case of the cake—Masterpiece Cakeshop, Ltd. v. Colorado Civil Rights Commission. In July 2012, a Lakewood, Colorado, baker declined to use his talent to create a custom wedding cake for a same-sex couple, two men. Same-sex marriage, the baker said, violated his Christian beliefs and his conscience. The two men quickly found another baker to make the cake they wanted, but they filed a complaint with the Colorado Civil Rights Commission. The Commission ordered the Christian baker to provide cakes for same-sex marriages, provide antidiscrimination training for his staff, and make quarterly reports for two years to the Commission demonstrating his compliance.

The baker refused to comply and instead chose not to make any wedding cakes at all—a decision he says cost him 40 percent of his business. Then he took the

Colorado Civil Rights Commission to court, claiming that the Commission had violated his rights to free speech and free exercise of religion under the First Amendment.

The Supreme Court agreed with the baker, ruling seven to two that the Commission had violated his First Amendment rights, and had done so out of bias against his religious beliefs. After that ruling, the baker returned to making wedding cakes.

The Supreme Court decision didn't stop anti-Christian forces from persecuting the Colorado baker. A transgender attorney later filed a civil suit against the baker for refusing to create a "gender-transition birthday cake." That case remains unresolved as I write these words—but this baker refuses to disobey his conscience or back down from the fight.

Second, there is the case of the Christian crisis pregnancy centers—National Institute of Family and Life Advocates v. Becerra. In California, the 2015 California Reproductive Freedom, Accountability, Comprehensive Care, and Transparency Act (also known as the FACT Act) required Christian crisis pregnancy centers to post notices advertising state-sponsored abortion clinics. Of course, crisis pregnancy centers exist to provide counseling and other assistance so that women can choose *not* to have an abortion.

Freedom of speech doesn't merely mean the freedom to speak your mind. It's also the freedom *not* to speak a message the government seeks to force on you. The free exercise clause of the First Amendment means that Christians have the freedom not just to worship as they please, but to put their beliefs into daily action.

The Christian crisis pregnancy centers lost their case in the famously far left Ninth Circuit Court of Appeals. But in June 2018, the Supreme Court of the United States ruled in a five-to-four decision that California's FACT Act violated the First Amendment.

Neither of these cases involved the right to worship. Instead, they involved our right to practice our faith and obey our religious conscience in our daily lives. I applaud the example of this Christian baker and these crisis pregnancy centers. At a high cost to themselves, they defended their right to think, believe, and behave as Christians in this post-Christian world.

The First Amendment was written to restrain the government from trampling on the human conscience. The government should never tell people what to think or what to believe or what to say. The government should never require people to violate their conscience for any reason. That's why religious freedom is the first right listed in the First Amendment.

Freedom of the Press—or Freedom to Suppress?

In *The Friends of Voltaire*, published in 1906, Evelyn Beatrice Hall (writing as S. G. Tallentyre) summarized the attitude of the French philosopher Voltaire toward his opponents: "I disapprove of what you say, but I will defend to the death your right to say it."[19] In these divided times, defending the First Amendment rights of opponents seems like a quaint idea. Yet the only way we can all be free is by respecting the freedom of others.

Freedom is more fragile than most of us realize. We

take our constitutional freedoms for granted—but they could be lost more quickly (and permanently) than we imagine. If we do not, as a society, respect the First Amendment rights of others, our civilization could collapse into chaos and mass insanity.

We saw America approaching this very brink in mid-2020, as days of protests turned into nights of arson, murder, and looting. In response to the lawlessness that had broken out across America, Senator Tom Cotton of Arkansas penned an opinion piece for the *New York Times*. Published on June 3, Cotton's op-ed read in part:

> Outnumbered police officers, encumbered by feckless politicians, bore the brunt of the violence. In New York State, rioters ran over officers with cars on at least three occasions. In Las Vegas, an officer is in "grave" condition after being shot in the head by a rioter. In St. Louis, four police officers were shot as they attempted to disperse a mob throwing bricks and dumping gasoline; in a separate incident, a 77-year-old retired police captain was shot to death as he tried to stop looters from ransacking a pawnshop. This is "somebody's granddaddy," a bystander screamed at the scene.

Senator Cotton urged the president to invoke the Insurrection Act and send the United States military to help the police and National Guard restore order.[20]

Scores of *Times* staffers openly revolted against Senator Cotton's opinion piece. Some claimed that the publication of the senator's views put the lives of *Times* employees in danger—though how mere words and ideas could pose such a threat was never explained.

Times publisher A. G. Sulzberger told angry staffers, "I believe in the principle of openness to a range of opinions, even those we may disagree with."[21] But the rebels at the *Times* wouldn't have it. They wanted only one viewpoint to be published by the *New York Times*: theirs.

In the ideology of "wokeness," opposing views cannot

> Freedom is more fragile than most of us realize.

be aired. They must be silenced. People who permit opposing views to be published must be fired. The radical staffers of the *New York Times* demanded a sacrifice—and they got it. James Bennet, the editor of the opinion page, was forced to resign.

Liberal writer Matt Taibbi of *Rolling Stone* was horrified by the uprising at the *Times*. In a piece called "The American Press Is Destroying Itself," Taibbi noted that at least seven other news organizations (including *The Intercept*, *Vox*, the *Philadelphia Inquirer*, and *Variety*) had suffered similar staff uprisings. These cases frequently involved staffers demanding the firing of colleagues. Taibbi compared these newsroom rebellions to the French Reign of Terror when cult leader Maximilien Robespierre and his "Committee of Public Safety" silenced all opposing views. Robespierre's committee sent more than seventeen thousand people to the guillotine (nicknamed "The Razor"). Taibbi wrote:

> We're watching an intellectual revolution....The American left has lost its mind. It's become a cowardly mob of upper-class social media addicts, Twitter Robespierres who move from discipline

to discipline, torching reputations and jobs with breathtaking casualness.

The leaders of this new movement are replacing traditional liberal beliefs about tolerance, free inquiry, and even racial harmony with ideas so toxic and unattractive that they eschew debate, moving straight to shaming, threats, and intimidation. They are counting on the guilt-ridden, self-flagellating nature of traditional American progressives, who will not stand up for themselves, and will walk to the Razor voluntarily.[22]

In July 2020, *New York Times* opinion editor Bari Weiss resigned her position, releasing a blistering letter denouncing the newspaper's coddling of its "woke" far-left staffers. In her letter, Weiss said that, at the *Times*, "intellectual curiosity—let alone risk-taking—is now a liability" and the cancel culture of Twitter has become the "ultimate editor" of the *Times*. She noted that she had been bullied by "woke" leftists who called her "a Nazi and a racist" and posted a threatening image of an ax by her name. "Showing up for work as a centrist at an American newspaper," she observed, "should not require bravery." She added that her experience showed that "lessons about the importance of understanding other Americans, the necessity of resisting tribalism, and the centrality of the free exchange of ideas to a democratic society" had "not been learned" at the *New York Times*.[23]

This is the age of the "call-out culture," the "cancel culture," and the "outrage culture," in which those who violate the constantly changing dogmas of the woke social justice warriors must be silenced, shamed, and "canceled" (shunned, silenced, and forced out of their careers). This is the brutal new reality of the post-Christian, post-Enlightenment "woke" era in which we live.

Blind to the Obvious

The First Amendment protects freedom of the press so that the people have the information they need to hold their elected officials accountable. Journalists used to take pride in accurately reporting the facts and letting their readers decide what to think. Those days are gone, and they've been gone for a long time.

In the early 1990s, far-left philosopher Noam Chomsky encouraged reporters to be boldly, unabashedly biased. He wrote,

> The *New York Times* plays an enormous role in shaping the perception of the current world....
> The *New York Times* creates history....
> Therefore it's extremely important if history is going to be shaped in an appropriate way, that certain things appear, certain things not appear, certain questions be asked, other questions be ignored, and that issues be framed in a particular fashion.... In fact, if the system functions well, it ought to have a liberal bias, or at least appear to.[24]

Today the *New York Times* is precisely the kind of leftist propaganda sheet that Chomsky envisioned, ignoring important questions while brazenly framing every issue according to a secular-left bias, and even forcing liberal editors like James Bennet to resign for not being "woke" enough.

But once Noam Chomsky got his wish, he apparently regretted it. In the wake of the *Times* revolt and the James Bennet resignation, Chomsky joined 152 other writers, artists, and academics in signing a letter warning that "the free exchange of information and ideas" was being threatened by "an intolerance of opposing views, a vogue for public shaming." That letter, titled "A Letter on Justice and Open Debate," was published on the *Harper's Magazine* website on July 7, 2020. Other signers included Gloria Steinem, Margaret Atwood, J. K. Rowling, Salman Rushdie, Fareed Zakaria, and Malcolm Gladwell. The response to the *Harper's* letter from the "woke" crowd was swift and brutal.[25] Chomsky and the other signers had stood up to the mob, and the mob responded by "canceling" them.

We live in a postmodern world in which journalists value "spin" over facts. They view objective truth as an illusion and think a radical "narrative" is more valid than truth. Across America, young, woke radicals are taking over America's newsrooms and strangling our First Amendment right to know the truth.

For example, during the rioting across America in May and June of 2020, KIRO-TV, the Seattle CBS affiliate, livestreamed the daylight looting of downtown Seattle shops and restaurants. All the windows of The Cheesecake Factory were shattered, and people walked off with bottles of wine and other items from the restaurant. As the KIRO news anchor talked live with the on-scene reporter, a woman walked out of The Cheesecake Factory with a cheesecake in her hands. The KIRO news anchor said, "You can see someone actually walking away with a cheesecake, there, after the Cheesecake

Factory was looted. Unclear where they may have gotten that."[26]

Read that last statement again: "Unclear where they may have gotten that." The woman just walked out of the Cheesecake Factory, yet it's unclear where she got the cheesecake? How can a professional news anchor deny the obvious facts in front of her eyes? As journalist Matt Taibbi lamented, "In a business where the first job requirement was once the willingness to ask tough questions, we've become afraid to ask obvious ones."[27]

The KIRO news anchor knew exactly where the woman got the cheesecake, but she couldn't bring herself to state the obvious. Why? I believe she mentally locked into the narrative that the rioters were striking a blow against oppression, and the looting was justified, noble, and beyond criticism. If that kind of thinking makes no sense to you, it's because you are not "woke." Unlike many in the media, you still have a grip on reality.

That same narrative about the noble looters gripped the majority of mainstream media. At the height of the riots, NBC News anchor Craig Melvin tweeted that his network would use misleading euphemisms to describe the rioting in Minneapolis: "This will guide our reporting in MN. 'While the situation on the ground in Minneapolis is fluid, and there has been violence, it is most accurate at this time to describe what is happening there as 'protests'—not riots.'"[28]

MSNBC reporter Ali Velshi stood in front of a burning building—that's right, a burning building—and said with a straight face, "This is mostly a protest. It is not, generally speaking, unruly, but fires have been started and this crowd is relishing that."[29]

Cheering the End of Civilization

In June 2020, rioters defaced and toppled numerous statues across America. At first, the vandals attacked statues of slave owners and Confederate generals. But it soon became apparent that, to the rioters, one statue was as good as another.

One image targeted by vandals was Philadelphia's statue of Matthias Baldwin, an opponent of slavery in the early 1800s. Baldwin also founded a school for Black children and fought for the right of Black Americans to vote. Yet vandals spray-painted "colonizer" and "murderer" across Baldwin's statue.[30]

In Whittier, California, the statue of Quaker abolitionist poet John Greenleaf Whittier was defaced with the spray-painted slogan "[Expletive] Slave Owners."[31]

And in San Francisco's Golden Gate Park, vandals spray-painted obscenities on the bust of sixteenth-century novelist Miguel de Cervantes, author of *Don Quixote*—a man who was captured by Barbary pirates and forced to work as a slave for five years in North Africa. "The great irony here," one reporter wrote about the vandalism, "is that Cervantes, unlike every person 'protesting' Cervantes' image, knew what it was like to be a slave."[32]

It goes to show that a mob has no morals, no intelligence, no reason, and no conscience. All the mob has is rage and passion and a remarkable ability to attack the wrong targets.

But the mobs are often cheered on by people who should know better. Amid the statue-destroying hysteria of mid-2020, CNN posted a story headlined, "Honoring the Unforgivable: The Horrific Acts Behind the Names on America's Infamous Monuments and Tributes."[33] CNN might as well have said, "Hey, rioters, here are some statues you missed! Come and get 'em!"

Then there's the ironic story of former ESPN and NBA analyst Chris Palmer. Tweeting from his California home on May 29, he posted a photo of a 189-unit affordable housing project in Minneapolis. The building was completely engulfed in flames due to the riots. Palmer's tweet read, "Burn that [expletive] down. Burn it all down."

Two days later, on May 31, Palmer tweeted, "They just attacked our sister community down the street. It's a gated community and they tried to climb the gates. They had to beat them back. Then [rioters] destroyed a Starbucks and are now in front of my building. Get these animals [euphemism] out of my neighborhood. Go back to where you live."[34] Palmer had cheered on the arsonists who burned down housing for the poor in Minneapolis, but when the rioters were on his doorstep, they were suddenly "animals."

I could go on for pages. The point is this: many in the mainstream media are acting like cheerleaders for the end of civilization. The First Amendment grants journalists the right to behave irresponsibly—but it also grants Americans the right to speak out and hold the media responsible.

Boldness to Speak the Truth

What can we do about the destructive narratives promoted by today's media? We can speak up. We can go to the contact page of our media outlets and praise them when they do a good job—and respectfully object when they promote a false narrative or attack our faith and values. We can organize and request to meet with media officials to present our views and complaints; the media can ignore individual emails but cannot ignore a chorus of many voices.

We can speak up on social media. But before we do, we need to make sure our facts are correct and well-sourced. We need to focus on lifting up Jesus and His gospel, not on tearing down this group or that individual. And we need to be ready for the "blowback" from the godless "cancel culture."

As Christians, we must not surrender our society to the secularists. We are in a battle for the future of our children and grandchildren. We fight this battle with prayer and obedience to God's Word. We don't believe in silencing our opponents. We believe in fighting bad ideas with better ideas. And the best ideas of all are found in God's Word.

The post-Christian times in which we live are very much like the early Christian era in the Book of Acts. The dominant culture hated Christianity and tried to stamp it out. In Acts 4, the priests, the temple guard, and the Sadducees (the political-religious sect that maintained the Jerusalem temple) arrested Peter and John as they preached in the temple courtyard. The next day, the guards hauled the two apostles before the Sanhedrin.

The rulers of the Sanhedrin ordered Peter and John to stop speaking in the name of Jesus—but the apostles refused to be silenced. They said, "Which is right in God's eyes: to listen to you, or to him? You be the judges! As for us, we cannot help speaking about what we have seen and heard" (vv. 19–20). Frustrated and enraged, the Sanhedrin threatened them again—then let them go.

The apostles had made some powerful enemies, and they had no First Amendment rights. They could have prayed, "Lord, stop these evil men! Silence them! Defeat them! Thwart their plans!" But that was not the prayer of Peter and John.

Instead, they prayed, "Now, Lord, consider their threats and enable your servants to speak your word with great boldness.

> We don't believe in silencing our opponents. We believe in fighting bad ideas with better ideas.

Stretch out your hand to heal and perform signs and wonders through the name of your holy servant Jesus" (vv. 29–30). They prayed for boldness!

Later, in Acts 5, the authorities arrested them again and said, "We gave you strict orders not to teach in this name. Yet you have filled Jerusalem with your teaching."

Peter and the other apostles replied, "We must obey God rather than human beings! The God of our ancestors raised Jesus from the dead—whom you killed by hanging him on a cross.... We are witnesses of these things, and so is the Holy Spirit, whom God has given to those who obey him" (vv. 28–30, 32).

The Sanhedrin had the apostles flogged and again ordered them not to speak in the name of Jesus. After the apostles were released, they continued to preach the gospel day after day—*with boldness.*

I believe we are heading into a time of severe testing. We are about to find out if we are made of the same stuff as the apostles. We are about to find out if we are willing to stand for God's truth, whatever the cost.

Friend in Christ, the Word of God is living and powerful, sharper than a double-edged sword, penetrating to the dividing of soul and spirit, joints and marrow; it judges the thoughts and attitudes of the heart. (See Hebrews 4:12.) In any contest of ideas, whether we have the First Amendment and Supreme Court on our side or our rights have been stripped from us and the entire world has risen against us—*God's truth will prevail.*

REFORM OUR SOCIETY

A FRIEND TOLD ME the story of a woman who hosted a sewing-oriented Facebook group for work-at-home moms. All members of the group agreed to one simple rule: only sewing-related topics may be posted on the group's Facebook page.

A few days after George Floyd died in Minneapolis police custody, a member of the Facebook group posted an anti-police video produced by a radical organization. The moderator of the Facebook group, who owned an online pattern business, removed the post and politely reminded members of the rules.

Activist members of the group were outraged. One woman demanded that the owner of the Facebook page state her opinion of the organization that produced the video—and she had better voice total support; otherwise, she was a racist, and no one should ever buy from her again. The Facebook group had to be shut down. A once-supportive community of mothers and grandmothers was torn apart by radical woke activism.

Increasingly radical activists are telling us not only what we can and can't say, but what we *must* say—or else. The radicals exert pressure to enforce one point of view, even though it's an extreme minority view. They allow no deviation, no nuance, no objection. Disagree with even one aspect of their agenda, and they will cancel you, shame you, and ruin you.

A New Reign of Terror

Around the same time as the Facebook page incident, twenty-eight-year-old David Shor, a progressive-leaning political scientist, was working for Civis Analytics, which does political consulting. As Shor watched peaceful protests turning into rampages of rioting and looting, he wondered about the political impact of the violence. He supported the cause and wanted the protests to be successful. He discovered research conducted by Omar Wasow of Princeton University, showing that violent protests tend to fail, but nonviolent protests tend to garner broad-based support.

When Shor tweeted these observations, the response was instantaneous and ruthless. Hashtag activists descended on Shor's Twitter account, denouncing him as a "racist" and "a vehicle for anti-blackness." One activist tweeted to Shor's employer, Civis Analytics, "Come get your boy"—and sure enough, Civis Analytics fired him. For trying to help the cause by telling the truth, he was attacked, mocked, shamed, and deprived of his livelihood.[1]

Wokeness is a religion. It has no God, but it has all the other trappings of a bullying, self-righteous, pharisaic religion. It demands absolute faith and mindless obedience. It has creeds and dogmas that no one dares to violate. Its doctrines can change without warning, and any who don't get the memo will be stoned as heretics.

People who transgress the rules of the wokeness religion may spend a lifetime atoning for their sin—but they'll never be forgiven. Wokeness is a religion without grace or mercy.

Like the inquisitions of the Middle Ages and the Salem witch trials of the 1690s, the wokeness religion torments its "heretics" until they confess. Like the Taliban dynamiting the Buddha statues of Bamian valley or ISIS bulldozing ancient monuments in Iraq and Syria,[2] the woke radicals have torn down statues and erased the past with wanton disregard for whether they've "canceled" a Confederate general or a Quaker abolitionist.

Social justice warriors may be a relatively new phenomenon in America, but the world has seen the same madness seizing control of a nation before. I refer to France in the late eighteenth century. The French Revolution was one of the "wokest" events in history. The revolutionaries, led by a cult figure named Maximilien Robespierre, claimed they wanted to end the privilege of the aristocracy, guarantee human rights and women's rights, and dismantle the church.

The French Revolution began with rioters beheading statues—the images of the twenty-eight kings of Judah carved over the door of the Notre Dame de Paris[3] (the ignorant mob thought they were French kings). But rioters soon went from beheading statues to beheading people. What began as a revolution quickly became a Reign of Terror—a bloodbath in which thousands died for the "crime" of being politically incorrect.

Could a Reign of Terror happen in America? Not only could it happen, *it has already begun.* Ordinary people are afraid to host a Facebook page for work-at-home moms. Reasonable, thoughtful progressives are branded "racists" and hounded out of their jobs for not being woke enough. The rational majority is being silenced by a comparatively small (but loud and violent) pack of radicals. The Reign of Terror is here, it's now, and it has spread across America faster than COVID-19. As Christians, we seek to be compassionate, reasonable, truthful, and charitable toward others, even the radicals. If they make a good point, we will honestly say, "That's a good point." But you can't reason with rioters. When the mob comes after you, your civility, compassion, and reason won't matter. They will brand you and destroy your reputation and try to get you fired. Or worse.

There will be very few people with the courage to stand by you and stick up for you because they know they're next in line to be "canceled." Why? Because this is America's Reign of Terror.

The Man Who Poisoned America

Where did "wokeness" and anti-American radicalism originate? Where did today's vast crop of anti-American radicals learn to despise America?

They learned it in the public schools paid for by our taxes. Most of all, they learned it from a man named Howard Zinn. He was a socialist who taught history and political science at Spelman College and Boston University. He wrote more than forty books, the most influential being *A People's History of the United States*, with some 2.6 million copies in print. First published in 1980, *A People's History* is still being updated, reprinted, and used to poison young minds today. It is widely used in Advanced Placement US history courses nationwide, which means that Zinn's distorted view of history is being force-fed to our brightest high school students.

As an Army Air Force bombardier in World War II, Zinn dropped napalm bombs over several European locations. After the war, he visited some of the cities he had bombed and learned about civilians who had died in those raids. Out of his guilt and resentment, along with his intense study of Marxist theories of class struggle, Zinn developed an oppressor-versus-victim narrative of American history.

Before Howard Zinn came along, we Americans saw ourselves as "We the People," a "melting pot" of many races, all working to build our dreams in a land of liberty, equal justice, and equal opportunity. The founding principle of the United States is the statement "all men are created equal." Since 1782, the American ideal of "E Pluribus Unum" ("Out of Many, One") has been enshrined on the Great Seal of the United States.

Over the years, we have often failed to live up to our ideals. The list of injustices in American history is long: slavery, the Dred Scott decision, the Trail of Tears, the brutal exploitation of Chinese immigrants, the Jim Crow era and segregation, the Tulsa massacre of 1921, the internment of Japanese Americans during World War II, and on and on. Because we are flawed human beings, we need our ideals, our statements of high principles, to keep drawing us toward equality, freedom, fairness, and righteousness. We need constant reminders that we are "one nation under God, indivisible, with liberty and justice for all."

Howard Zinn was determined to replace this view of

America with his narrative of America-as-oppressor. In the opening chapter of *A People's History of the United States*, Zinn makes it clear that his book is an assault on traditional American ideals, which he calls a "pretense." He wrote:

> The pretense is that there really is such a thing as "the United States," subject to occasional conflicts and quarrels, but fundamentally a community of people with common interests....
>
> My viewpoint, in telling the history of the United States, is different....Nations are not communities and never have been. The history of any country, presented as the history of a family, conceals fierce conflicts of interest (sometimes exploding, most often repressed) between conquerors and conquered, masters and slaves, capitalists and workers, dominators and dominated in race and sex.[4]

So Zinn created a *new* narrative of American history, rooted in Marxist theories of class struggle—a narrative that denies the validity of America's founding doctrines and principles. He set out to write a version of American history as seen through the lens of a toxic bias.

But Zinn had a problem. As John Adams, one of the Founding Fathers, said, "Facts are stubborn things."[5] American history didn't conform to Zinn's predetermined narrative. Yes, there were periods in which oppressors mistreated victims, in which masters bought and sold slaves, in which bosses exploited workers. All other American history books acknowledged these injustices.

But Zinn didn't want his readers to see these injustices as mere episodes in American history. He intended to *completely redefine* America as *evil* in the minds of his readers. He wanted to topple all the great heroes of American history and portray them as villains: Christopher Columbus, George Washington and all the Founding Fathers, and even Abraham Lincoln. Princeton history professor Sean Wilentz offered this assessment of Zinn's approach to history.

> What he did was take all of the guys in white hats and put them in black hats, and vice versa.... To see history as a battleground of warring perspectives is to abandon the seat of reason.
>
> He saw history primarily as a means to motivate people to political action that he found admirable. That's what he said he did. It's fine as a form of agitation—agitprop [political agitation propaganda]—but it's not particularly good history....
>
> Abraham Lincoln freed the slaves. You wouldn't know that from Howard Zinn.[6]

And Roger Kimball, author of *Tenured Radicals: How Politics Has Corrupted Higher Education*, observed, "Zinn's book has probably done more to poison the minds of high school students than any other work of history."[7] Even students who have never read *A People's History of the United States* have been infected by its ideas through other Zinn-influenced curricula and books, through teachers, and the media. Zinn's toxic influence on American society has been pervasive.

In 2019, historian Mary Grabar published *Debunking Howard Zinn: Exposing the Fake History That Turned a Generation against America.* In that book, she documents the destructive impact Zinn's textbook has had on millions of impressionable minds. In an interview for the Alexander Hamilton Institute, she talked about what she had learned in writing the book:

> I knew *A People's History of the United States* was terrible. Indeed, most people, unless they are young or otherwise impressionable, can see how slanted the book is in the opening pages.
>
> But as I researched more deeply my suspicions turned to shock. Not only does Zinn put a far-left spin on events in American history, but he uses illegitimate sources (ideological New Left historians, a socialist novelist, a Holocaust-denying historian), plagiarizes, misrepresents authors' words, leaves out critical information, and presents outright lies....
>
> Simply put, Zinn's *People's History of the United States* is probably the biggest con job in American history writing ever.[8]

Grabar discovered that, in his treatment of Christopher Columbus, Zinn plagiarized passages from a book by far-left writer Hans Koning. He also selectively quoted from Columbus's diaries to falsely portray him as a greedy, heartless slave trader. An honest reading of Columbus' diaries reveals him as a devout Christian who was concerned for the welfare of the Native Americans he encountered. For example, Zinn omitted this journal entry by Columbus: "I know that [Native Americans] are a people who can be made free and converted to our Holy Faith more by love than by force." Zinn also omitted entries regarding Columbus' orders to his sailors to treat the Native Americans with kindness.[9]

Zinn presents a false view of Native Americans before the arrival of Columbus, portraying them as living idyllic, peaceful lives. In fact, Native American tribes waged war against each other and enslaved each other for centuries prior to the arrival of Europeans. Zinn's libelous history is the primary reason many have pushed in recent years to have Columbus Day replaced with Indigenous Peoples' Day across America—and the reason angry mobs pulled down statues of Columbus in 2020. The truth about Columbus didn't fit Zinn's hate-America narrative, so Zinn lied—and millions of Americans have bought the lie.

Zinn wrote the first edition of *A People's History of the United States* just a few years after the Vietnam War and Watergate. America appeared to be in decline, and many Americans were cynical about their nation's future. Most American movies were pessimistic tales of antiheroes and American failure: *The Godfather, All the President's Men, Taxi Driver, The Deer Hunter, Apocalypse Now.* The education establishment was primed to embrace a textbook portraying America as a cancer on human history.

As Zinn's oppressor-victim narrative gained a foothold in American education, more and more people accepted it. The idea soon created pressure for everyone to conform. Zinn's narrative and its corollary lies—"America is a racist nation," "Columbus was a genocidal murderer," "Lincoln didn't care about freeing the slaves"—have become a cascade of delusion that drives public policy, education, the media, politics, and the violence of street rioters. Zinn's narrative has turned America's melting pot into a boiling cauldron of bitterness and hate.

A People's History of the United States has been continuously poisoning young minds for forty years. Suppose you spent four solid decades indoctrinating class after class of students in the notion that America is fundamentally evil and oppressive. What effect would you expect to see in American society?

In the media, you would expect to see biased reporters continually telling us how racist and oppressive America is. You'd expect to see both secular-left progressives and progressive Christians condemning America. You'd expect to see screaming mobs tearing down statues of Christopher Columbus and George Washington. You'd expect to see popular sports figures kneeling instead of respecting the national anthem. You'd expect to see radical groups calling for the elimination of all police departments.

Today we see all that and more. Much of the upheaval in our society is rooted in the false narrative Howard Zinn has injected into millions of young minds. Tax-paying parents thought their kids were learning American history. Instead, their kids were being indoctrinated in a false, Marxist-inspired narrative.

Is America a fundamentally evil, oppressive society that must be burned down to its foundation? Or can the founding principles of America enable us to right wrongs, heal wounds, and create a just and free society? Because of the viral infection of Zinn's libelous narrative, many young people just want to burn it down.

In 1862, during the depths of the Civil War, Abraham Lincoln told Congress, "We shall nobly save, or meanly lose, the last best hope of earth."[10] For all its flaws and past sins, it was America that first declared "all men are created equal." It was America that abolished slavery—an evil institution still practiced in other parts of the world today, notably in Communist China. It is America that millions (including myself) have immigrated to in search of freedom and equality.

When Lincoln dedicated the Civil War cemetery at Gettysburg, Pennsylvania, he reminded us that America was "conceived in Liberty and dedicated to the proposition that all men are created equal." In our generation, we must renew our commitment to that proposition. We must stand against the lie that America was founded to perpetuate oppression and slavery when the exact opposite is true. And we must seek God's guidance and protection so that "this nation, under God, shall have a new birth of freedom—and that government of the people, by the people, for the people, shall not perish from the earth."[11]

Critical Theory

In chapter 1, I talked about a phenomenon that sociologists call an information cascade or an availability cascade. I call it a "delusion cascade"—a false and destructive notion that spreads like a virus through masses of people, becoming a self-reinforcing collective belief.

One of the most destructive delusions that has infected Western society is a Marxist-inspired body of thought known as critical theory. There are several "flavors" of this theory—critical race theory, critical gender theory, critical legal theory, and more. Even though

Marxism has failed every time it's been tried, today's Marxist radicals keep spreading their poisonous ideas in an effort to take over the world.

Classical Marxism divided people into economic classes—the wealthy oppressors versus the oppressed workers. The problem for today's Marxists is that dividing people into economic classes doesn't work. American freedom enabled poor people to move up the economic ladder. A poor person could start a business in America and become a rich person.

Since the Marxists couldn't start a revolution in America based on class warfare, they decided to divide people by race, gender, sexuality, and so forth, and then set them at war with each other. They would do this by convincing people that they were victims of "systemic oppression." This is called "awakening" people to "critical consciousness." Once a person realizes that he or she is a victim of oppression, that person has been awakened—and is now "woke."[12]

The victim-oppressor narrative of critical theory does not *solve* racism—it *perpetuates* racism even while calling itself antiracism. Critical theory claims that America, free market capitalism, the police, and the church are all irredeemably and fundamentally racist. It teaches that racism is unsolvable, and that people are incapable of changing. European Americans are born racist and will always be racist. This is a message of such books as Robin DiAngelo's *White Fragility* and Ibram X. Kendi's *How to Be an Antiracist*.

The victim-oppressor narrative of critical theory drives all the forces that are seeking to destroy Western civilization:

- The riots and looting in our streets
- The revolt and unrest on our university campuses
- The millionaire basketball players who disrespect the American flag
- The "defund the police" movement among the radical left
- The millions of American schoolchildren, from kindergartners to high school seniors, who are taught to hate America
- The *New York Times*' 1619 Project, which teaches that America was not founded in 1776 to establish freedom and human rights, but was founded when the first African slaves came to America in 1619

All of these destructive forces, and many more, can be traced back to critical theory, which has seized control of most of our major universities. It began in the law schools and spread to the ethnic studies and gender studies departments. Today critical theory infects almost every educational discipline in many universities, from history to music theory to mathematics.

James Lindsay, a mathematics professor from Portland State University, told of getting into a Twitter war with "woke" radicals over the question "Does two plus two always equal four?" One person on Twitter who claimed to be a teacher, scholar, and "social justice change agent" insisted that two plus two equals four is *not* an objective fact, but a "cultural" notion resulting from "Western imperialism" and "colonization." And a councilperson for the Washington state Ethnic Studies program claimed that, in some cultures, two plus two might actually equal five! She put out a call to her Twitter followers: "How can we turn this [two plus two equals five] into a true statement?"

To the "woke" activists, the mere existence of objective truth is a form of oppression. If the advocates of critical theory can deconstruct such an obvious truth as two plus two equals four, they can deconstruct *any* truth.

Lindsay observed that today's critical theory woke activism is a fulfillment of the prophetic novel *Nineteen Eighty-Four*, in which George Orwell wrote, "In the end the Party would announce that two and two made five, and you would have to believe it. It was inevitable that they should make that claim sooner or later: the logic of their position demanded it."[13]

The woke activists are using tactics of violence and intimidation to force all of us to accept the false tenets of critical theory. In city after city, roving bands of activists invade restaurants, ordering patrons to chant slogans, raise their fists, or fall on their knees. To frighten people into compliance, the activists overturn tables, smash glass, scream slogans, and swing skateboards at people. (It must be noted that in video after video of these attacks, most of the activists are White radicals, not Black people.)[14]

In the days to come, you and I may face violence and intimidation from radical activists who despise the truth. They may confront us in a restaurant, on the street, or even in church. They may demand that we raise our fists or chant some slogan or kneel before them. They may threaten us with injury or death if we don't comply. You have to make the decision whether or not you will submit to their threats—or take a stand for Christ.

I have already decided what I'm going to say if I'm ever in such a situation. I plan to respond, "I kneel only to King Jesus. He alone is the solution to racism. Jesus is Lord."

The Delusion Cascade

The pressure to conform to the secular-left, anti-American agenda has become unbelievably intense.

Case in point: During the May–June 2020 riots, a progressive-leaning investigative reporter, Lee Fang of *The Intercept*, tweeted an interview with an African American man known as Maximum Fr. In the interview, the man said, "Why does a Black life matter only when a white man takes it?...Like, if a white man takes my life tonight, it's going to be national news, but if a Black man takes my life, it might not even be spoken of."[15]

Lee Fang was immediately barraged by angry tweets, including one from an *Intercept* coworker who tweeted, "Tired of being made to deal with my coworker @lhfang continuing to push narratives about black on black crime after being repeatedly asked not to"[16] and then commented, "Stop being racist Lee."[17] Vicious tweets from other (mostly white) journalists at *The Intercept*, the *New York Times*, and MSNBC also accused Fang of racism. Only one journalist, Matt Taibbi, was willing to defend Lee Fang. He wrote:

> Like many reporters, Fang has always viewed it as part of his job to ask questions in all directions.

He's written critically of political figures on the center-left, the left, and "obviously on the right," and his reporting has inspired serious threats in the past. None of those past experiences were as terrifying as this blitz by would-be colleagues, which he described as "jarring," "deeply isolating," and "unique in my professional experience."...

[Lee Fang] appears earnestly committed to making the world a better place through his work. It's stunning that so many colleagues are comfortable using a word as extreme and villainous as *racist* to describe him.[18]

That is how a delusion cascade works. It uses fear to reinforce a narrative that everyone *must* buy into. Truth is slain on the altar of the delusional narrative. Anyone who contradicts this narrative will be canceled and publicly shamed as a racist.

Public shaming not only punishes the "offenders" like Lee Fang. It sends a message throughout the culture: *If you step out of line, the same fate will befall you.* Political correctness is brutally enforced. Fear reigns supreme.

The radicals have rigged the national conversation in such a way that they win every argument. They portray everyone who opposes their agenda as racist, sexist, misogynist, or homophobic. Their targets are people who believe in logic and reason, democracy, traditional American values, Western civilization, and the Judeo-Christian faith tradition.

They have hijacked the language, using the same words you and I use, but with different meanings. This is a deliberate strategy to get us to agree to their goals and their agenda without realizing what we are doing. They say, "We believe in social justice!" We say, "We believe in social justice too." But what they mean and what we mean are two different things.

In the Western democratic tradition, *social justice* means a condition in which all people are treated fairly and given equal opportunity to achieve their goals, and the poor are treated with compassion and dignity. But to the radicals, *social justice* means a condition in which so-called "oppressors" are overthrown, and resources are redistributed in accordance with the theories of Karl Marx. The radicals believe it is permissible to commit crimes—looting, rioting, killing, burning—to achieve so-called "social justice."

During the protests and riots of mid-2020, many evangelical leaders and pastors demonstrated support for a far-left organization on their websites and social media. If they had read the "What We Believe" statement posted on the organization's website, they would have learned that the organization opposes the "Western-prescribed nuclear family structure."[19] As Christians, we know that the key to having successful, fulfilled lives is a strong, intact family—the kind of family God prescribed in Genesis 2. Intact, two-parent families produce children who are better equipped to succeed in school and life. But this radical organization seeks to destroy the family.

One of the founders of this far-left organization has publicly stated, "We are trained Marxists. We are super versed on ideological theories."[20] One goal of Marxists is to overturn the American economic system, the American system of government, and the American way of life. So the evangelical pastors and leaders who supported this organization were, in fact, aiding and abetting the downfall of the family and Western civilization. These Christians had not done their homework. Their hearts may have been in the right place, but their heads were under the sand.

I believe Satan uses delusion cascades and peer pressure to spread his lies and silence opposition. The notion that we must obey the narrative instead of the truth has darkened human hearts throughout our culture. It has hardened human hearts not only to the truth about America but the truth of the gospel.

Jesus said, "If you hold to my teaching, you are really my disciples. Then you will know the truth, and the truth will set you free.... So if the Son sets you free, you will be free indeed."[21] But cascades of delusion have blinded our culture to all truth, including the truth of the gospel. The radical false narrative enslaves our nation with chains of rage and bitterness.

Only God's truth will set America free.

Taking Freedom for Granted

I was born into the ancient Christian community of Egypt, which was founded in Alexandria by Mark the evangelist in the first century AD, just a few years after the resurrection of Jesus. I grew up in Egypt during a time of great oppression under the regime of President Gamal Abdel Nasser, the founder of the Arab Socialist Union. Nasser stoked the fires of Islamic hostility toward Christians. He clamped down on churches and enacted laws that severely restricted the rights of Christians.

During the Nasser years, no new churches could be built without the permission of the head of state. No evangelism or missionary work was permitted outside church walls. Some of those laws are still enforced in Egypt today.

Nasser increased the number of informants to the point that you never knew who might be a government spy. In the marketplace, at the university, and on the street, no one dared to speak a critical word of President Nasser or the government. Even in the privacy of their own homes, people spoke in whispers, fearing an informant might be listening at the window or on the other side of the apartment wall.

Growing up in an era of fear and repression, I was an American in my heart long before I ever set foot on American soil. I yearned for freedom, and I viewed America as the repository of everything I desperately longed for: liberty, equality, and opportunity. I dreamed of moving to America and becoming an American citizen. Most of all, I dreamed of enjoying the freedom to speak my mind and exercise my religion without fear of being arrested.

When I checked books on America out of the library, I worried that someone might report me to the Egyptian government. I feared that the state security agency might interrogate me about my interest in America. Despite my fears, I couldn't stop reading and dreaming of America. In 1977, I realized my dream and moved to the United States, and in 1984, I achieved my goal of becoming a US citizen.

Upon my arrival in America, I was dismayed to discover how many Americans had so little regard for their history and the blessings of freedom they enjoyed. This disregard for America's legacy of freedom is even more widespread today than it was then.

Having just moved from a repressive socialist dictatorship, I had a perspective on freedom that many native-born Americans didn't have. Many who had lived in America all their lives couldn't imagine what a privilege it was to live here. They had always been free to speak out, to vote, and to talk openly about their religious faith. They took freedom for granted. Because I grew up in a land of fear and repression, I never take freedom for granted.

Why don't people dream of finding a better life in North Korea? Somalia? Venezuela? Iran? Syria? Why aren't huddled masses of refugees eager to emigrate to those nations? The question answers itself: There is neither freedom nor economic opportunity (the byproduct of freedom) in those countries. People are desperate to escape *from* those countries. No one is trying to sneak *into* those countries.

America attracts immigrants because America is the land of liberty. One of our most precious American freedoms is the right to speak the truth without fear of punishment or arrest. At one time, this freedom was a fact of American life, as fixed and unassailable as Mount Rushmore. But there are growing numbers of people today who want to take away those rights—and they also want to do away with Mount Rushmore!

Freedom in America is under assault as never before.

Is There Hope for America?

The death of freedom always begins with the abolition of truth and oppression of those who speak it. It is hypocrisy for any person or group to demand their own right to free speech even as they trample the First Amendment rights of others. Free speech creates a marketplace for ideas, not an excuse to shame or to bully or "cancel" those who think differently.

As I have watched the rioting and rage gripping America these days, I have reminded the members of my congregation that every person is made in the image of God—African American and European American, police officer and protester, atheist and evangelist. All are made in God's image, and all are individuals. We must not prejudge people because of the color of their skin or the uniform they wear.

We cannot deny that many Americans of color have suffered greatly because of racism and unequal treatment. Though our Founding Fathers endeavored to build a society based on the principle that all human beings are created equal by God, we have undeniably fallen short of that goal.

> Every person is made in the image of God— African American and European American, police officer and protester, atheist and evangelist.

Americans are a flawed people. America is an imperfect nation, but America is not an oppressive nation. It is still a land of opportunity. It hurts me deeply to know that many people limit themselves by believing the lie that America is victimizing them and holding them down because of their skin color. America is still a melting pot of races and ethnicities, a nation that still strives to form a more perfect union. America has never claimed perfection but has always pursued justice and equality.

But we have arrived at a tipping point in American history—and we could go either way. We could return to the founding principles that made our society great— or we could tumble into the same abyss that has swallowed so many nations and empires over the centuries.

Many of our leaders are actively pushing our society toward the abyss. In response to a howling band of extreme-left radicals representing the thinnest sliver of the American population, our cities are buckling and "defunding the police," collaborating in the collapse of civilization. Reasonable, civilized taxpayers vastly outnumber the radical mob—but it's the radicals who rule the day.

> America is still a melting pot of races and ethnicities, a nation that still strives to form a more perfect union. America has never claimed perfection but has always pursued justice and equality.

It's up to you and me to speak out and to pray fervently, asking God to spare America and bring revival. During times of great national pain and crisis, we need to remember our founding principles. We need to remember who we are as Americans. And we in the church need to remember who we are called to be as Christians.

In our darkest moments as a nation, America has always relied on its moral and spiritual foundation to keep from sliding too far. Even when our leaders were caught up in scandals, America's moral foundation was strong enough to withstand the shock. Today, however, America's moral and spiritual foundation is crumbling, and we're approaching the point of no return. As our leaders and our people reject God's law and forsake America's moral foundation, there is no guardrail in place to keep us from tumbling into the abyss.

When a nation abandons God and His law, the next stop is utter darkness. But even at this late hour, I believe there is still hope.

We must get serious about obeying God's law. We must get serious about falling to our knees and confessing our sins, praying for our nation and our leaders, and pleading with God to raise up godly leaders who can point the way out of the darkness. We must get serious about praying for our church leaders and holding them accountable for preaching the uncompromised truth of God's Word. The old saying is true: "As goes the pulpit, so goes the pew, and as goes the pew, so goes the nation."

> **When a nation abandons God and His law, the next stop is utter darkness. But even at this late hour, I believe there is still hope.**

In his Lyceum address in 1838, twenty-eight-year-old Abraham Lincoln spoke these words of warning—and, I fear, prophecy:

> All the armies of Europe, Asia and Africa combined, with all the treasure of the earth...could not by force, take a drink from the Ohio, or make a track on the Blue Ridge, in a trial of a thousand years.

At what point then is the approach of danger to be expected? I answer, if it ever reach us, it must spring up amongst us.[22]

I believe Lincoln's words are true—and I fear they are being fulfilled before our eyes. The threat that is dragging our civilization to ruin is here. I don't merely mean the radicals who riot in the streets and tear down statues; I mean our cowardly leaders' surrender to the radicals' demands. And I mean the pastors and churches that have fallen all over themselves to side with the radicals as society comes apart at the seams.

Is there no hope? Is America doomed to go the way of lost Babylon and the fallen Roman Empire? Are our children and grandchildren condemned to grow up in a ruined, post-American world? I don't believe it's too late for America—not yet.

It's not too late to bow before God and plead for our nation. It's not too late for God to hear and answer from heaven. It's not too late for revival to sweep our land. I don't want to leave you despairing for America's future, so please turn the page and read on with me—and discover how you can play a part in saving America for future generations.

REVIVE THE CHURCH

I N JUNE 2020, as America was under assault by roving bands of rioters obsessed with destroying statues and erasing history, one radical activist tweeted that statues of Jesus that depicted Him as a "white European" should "come down.... Tear them down."[1]

It's true that Jesus was not a white European. He was born a Jew, a descendant of King David—yet He truly belongs to the world, to every race, ethnicity, and nation on earth. He has been represented in art with Middle Eastern features, with Black African features, with Asian features, Latino features, and on and on. Jesus belongs to the entire human race.

You've undoubtedly heard a beautiful Christmas song called "Some Children See Him," written in 1951 by jazz composer Alfred Burt and lyricist Wilha Hutson. The song says that some children see Jesus as "lily white," others see Him "bronzed and brown," and others see Him as "almond-eyed." Every child can see himself or herself reflected in the loving eyes of Jesus. As the hymn by John Oxenham reminds us:

> In Christ there is no east or west,
> In him no south or north,

But one great fam'ly bound by love
Throughout the whole wide earth.[2]

Anyone who advocates mob violence against churches has aligned himself with evil and hate. Certainly, this radical must know that once the mob begins tearing down statues, it will soon move on to tearing down crosses and entire churches. The notion of attacking churches and desecrating symbols of Jesus could only come from one source. As the apostle Paul tells us: "The god of this age has blinded the minds of unbelievers, so that they cannot see the light of the gospel that displays the glory of Christ, who is the image of God" (2 Cor. 4:4).

The Marxist-inspired "woke" radicals have proven that they seek the destruction of the church and the eradication of the Christian gospel. In August 2020, after two continuous months of protests and violent riots in the city of Portland, Oregon, rioters vented their rage against the Word of God. Activists holding signs reading "Black Lives Matter" gathered in front of Portland's federal building and set fire to a stack of Bibles.

A witness to the Bible-burning, Ian Cheong, recorded the incident and posted the video online. "Left-wing activists bring a stack of Bibles to burn in front of the federal courthouse in Portland," Cheong wrote, adding, "I don't know what burning the Bible has to do with protesting against police brutality. Do not be under the illusion that these protests and riots are anything but an attempt to dismantle all of Western Civilization and upend centuries of tradition and freedom of religion."[3]

Jesus told us to expect persecution—and He told us to love our enemies. The Lord loves even the radicals who attack His church. We love them with the love of Jesus and pray the prayer Jesus prayed from the cross— "Father, forgive them; for they know not what they do."[4]

We can only heal our society and our nation through Christlike love and grace.

Needed: Gladiators, Not Onlookers

We Christians are law-abiding people. When the COVID-19 virus invaded our land, we complied with government orders. We closed our churches. We sheltered at home, physically cut off from our fellow believers, but maintaining our fellowship through Facebook or Zoom or YouTube.

We couldn't help noticing that while we obeyed orders to close our churches, abortion clinics and pot dispensaries remained open. The streets were filled with protesters, rioters, and vandals tearing down statues, and the government didn't respond. But churches, the government said, had to stay closed. I think we are only seeing the beginning of the unfair treatment and persecution that lies ahead for the church.

As it becomes more risky and costly to be a follower of Jesus in our society, we need to look to the example of the early apostles. We need to respond to threats, injustice, oppression, and persecution as they did. How did they respond? They didn't pray for safety. They didn't pray for an easy life. No, they prayed for boldness. They prayed for the courage to speak God's truth.

And when their persecutors tried to silence them, they answered, "We must obey God rather than human beings!" The time is now upon us when we must pray for boldness rather than safety. We must obey God rather than human beings. The time of testing for the church and God's people has begun.

In this time of testing, you are not alone. When you were told to shelter at home, when your church closed its doors, when you had minimal human contact, I'm sure you often felt alone. And when the radicals rioted in the streets, and the government praised them and welcomed them and allowed them to burn buildings and tear down statues without consequences, you probably felt alone. You felt alone in your values and principles, your love of country, your respect for the law, and your faith in Jesus Christ.

> **The time is now upon us when we must pray for boldness rather than safety. We must obey God rather than human beings.**

I don't believe, as some conspiracy theorists suggest, that the lockdown of churches was a deliberate scheme by some shadowy group to isolate Christians from one another. But I do believe that Satan is trying to exploit this pandemic for his purposes. I believe he seeks to silence and weaken and discourage the church. It's a strategy the apostle Paul described when he wrote, "For our struggle is not against flesh and blood, but against the rulers, against the authorities, against the powers of this dark world and against the spiritual forces of evil in the heavenly realms" (Eph. 6:12).

Satan and his forces want you to be afraid, want you to feel isolated and fearful, want you to be ineffective for Christ in these crucial days. As Christians, we must stand united, praying fervently and speaking boldly. The Lord Jesus may return before you finish reading this sentence—or He may return ten thousand years from now. It's not up to us to know the times and schedules of God's eternal plan. Our job is to keep working in His fields, reaping a harvest of souls. May the Lord find us boldly proclaiming His gospel when He returns.

As I write these words, our nation is in flames, and our culture appears to be collapsing. It seems that our future hangs by the slenderest thread. In a cultural and spiritual catastrophe of this magnitude, no one can be a spectator. We need gladiators in the arena, not onlookers in the stands. All Christians must report for duty.

Taking Enemy-Held Territory for God

There are human rulers in this world who are enjoying the meltdown of Western society. I can picture the dictators of Russia and China, along with the ayatollahs of the Muslim world, all rubbing their hands together with glee as they see images of American cities in upheaval and crisis.

But those human rulers are not the real rulers of this world. They are mere servants and lackeys of the true god of this age, who is Satan. You may say, "I don't want to have to deal with Satan! Can't I just ignore him? Can't I pretend he doesn't exist?" No, you can't. Satan would like you to pretend he doesn't exist. He's probably most successful when he deludes people into thinking he is not real.

Satan seeks to catch us unprepared for the spiritual battle. Demons fight dirty. They know all our weak points and vulnerabilities. My friend, you may not be interested in Satan, but Satan is interested in you. You can't simply ignore him. You must prepare yourself for battle.

When Jesus began His ministry, He went out into the wilderness, where Satan attacked Him and tried to destroy Him. Every time Satan attacked, Jesus defeated him through the wisdom of Scripture. If Satan didn't hesitate to attack Jesus the Master, he won't hesitate to attack Jesus' followers, you and me. That's why Paul tells us, "Finally, be strong in the Lord and in his mighty power" (Eph. 6:10).

> It's not up to us to know the times and schedules of God's eternal plan. Our job is to keep working in His fields, reaping a harvest of souls. May the Lord find us boldly proclaiming His gospel when He returns.

We cannot defeat Satan in our own wisdom and strength. So Paul tells us, "Therefore put on the full armor of God, so that when the day of evil comes, you may be able to stand your ground, and after you have done everything, to stand" (Eph. 6:13). Our enemies are spiritual forces, and we need spiritual armor. We can only stand our ground if we are fully armored for spiritual warfare. Paul tells us that the armor of God consists of six items:

> Stand firm then, with the belt of truth buckled around your waist, with the breastplate of righteousness in place, and with your feet fitted with the readiness that comes from the gospel of peace.

In addition to all this, take up the shield of faith, with which you can extinguish all the flaming arrows of the evil one. Take the helmet of salvation and the sword of the Spirit, which is the word of God.

—EPHESIANS 6:14–17

Let's look at each of the six components of the full armor of God.

First, there is the *belt of truth*. In Paul's day, soldiers wore a wide leather belt around the waist. A Christian who is not encircled by God's truth, as revealed in Scripture, will fall for Satan's lies. Ignorance and indifference to God's truth leave us wide open to the attacks of Satan.

> We need gladiators in the arena, not onlookers in the stands. All Christians must report for duty.

Second, there is the *breastplate of righteousness*. Roman soldiers wore a plate of metal armor to protect the vital organs of the chest, especially the heart. The breastplate of righteousness protects us in much the same way. Jesus completed our salvation on the cross, and Satan can never steal the Lord's righteousness from us. Satan will attack us with doubts about our salvation and accusations regarding our sins. But we are covered by the righteousness of Jesus. The Word of God promises us, "There is now no condemnation for those who are in Christ Jesus" (Rom. 8:1). When you go into spiritual battle, make sure you are wearing your bulletproof breastplate of righteousness.

Third, your *feet must be fitted with the gospel of peace*. The image here is of a soldier whose feet are shod, who is ready to leap into action and hit the ground running. The gospel, the good news of Jesus Christ, compels us to invade enemy territory and to take that territory for Him. The gospel of peace is the irrefutable truth that, through Christ and Christ alone, we now have peace with God and peace with one another. With the gospel of peace on our feet, we are not afraid of any enemy, whether spiritual or human.

Fourth, there is the *shield of faith*. Roman soldiers often went into battle carrying a full-body shield, about five feet high and almost three feet wide. Made of wood and clad in metal, a Roman shield could deflect the flaming arrows of the enemy. If an unshakable faith in Jesus Christ shields you, the flaming darts of Satan cannot harm you.

Fifth, there is the *helmet of salvation*. The symbolism of the helmet is obvious. The helmet protects the brain, the seat of the human mind and soul. Satan is a master psychologist, and he attacks us in the realm of the mind. He seeks to twist our emotions and distort our thinking. He tries to make us doubt God's Word and tempt us into disobedience and sin. Don't go into battle without your helmet! Remember, you are saved by grace through faith and not through your works. Trust the salvation that Jesus purchased for you on the cross, and He will protect your mind from Satan's attack.

Sixth, there is the *sword of the Spirit, which is the Word of God*. You may have noticed that all the other items of our spiritual armor are for defensive use. They are protective, but they are not weapons. The sword of the Spirit is different. A sword is both an offensive and defensive weapon. You can use it to attack the enemy— but you can also use it to fend off the enemy's blows. This is why it's so important to commit Scripture to memory. The more Scripture we know, the better prepared we'll be for Satan's attacks.

The Word of God is a sword that cuts through the arguments and defenses of worldly people. The Word of God pierces the conscience and awakens the souls of those who are spiritually dead. If we have fed our minds on God's Word, the Spirit will be able to speak His Word to us and through us.

Did you notice there's one part of the warrior's body that the full armor of God doesn't cover? Paul says nothing about armor for the warrior's back. I believe that's deliberate. God, speaking through Paul, wants us to know that there is no protection for running away. Never turn your back on the devil. If you run from the battle, your back will be exposed to the enemy. The only safety lies in advancing toward the enemy—belt and breastplate fastened, feet shod, helmet in place, shield raised, sword in hand. Fully armored, we can assault the gates of hell—and prevail.

In these turbulent times, in this present crisis, you and I need the full armor of God as never before. And even though these days often seem frightening, I can honestly say that I am glad to be alive in these exciting times. Yes, I'm concerned for my children and grandchildren and the many young Christians who are growing up in these perilous times. But I also believe God has granted us the privilege of seeing Him demonstrate His might and power through the upheaval of these days.

Troubled times give us an opportunity to know Christ more fully and to make Him known to the people around us. In the entire history of the world, there has never been a crisis like this—or an opportunity like this. The Lord has flung wide the door of opportunity to pro claim His love to the world.

The battle of a lifetime has come upon us, and we must wade into it, armored head to toe, wielding the mighty sword of the Spirit, the Word of God. We must be like those Allied soldiers on D-Day, June 6, 1944, who leaped out of the landing craft and waded ashore onto the beaches of Normandy. We must put our bodies on the line and conquer enemy-held territory for the kingdom of God.

Troubled times give us an opportunity to know Christ more fully and to make Him known to the people around us.

The Social Media Arena

Sam Harris is a prominent spokesman for atheism, so there is very little on which he and I would agree. But we do see eye-to-eye on one thing: the destructive power of social media. In a podcast in 2020, Harris said:

> Conversation is the only tool we have for making progress, I firmly believe that. But many of the things we most need to talk about, seem impossible to talk about.
>
> I think social media is a huge part of the problem. I've been saying for a few years now that, with social media, we've all been enrolled in a

psychological experiment for which no one gave consent, and it's not at all clear how it will turn out....All information is becoming weaponized. All communication is becoming performative. And on the most important topics, it now seems to be fury and sanctimony and bad faith almost all the time.

We appear to be driving ourselves crazy. Actually, crazy. As in, incapable of coming into contact with reality, unable to distinguish fact from fiction....Almost everyone with a public platform is terrified. Journalists, and editors, and executives, and celebrities are terrified that they might take one wrong step here, and never recover.

And this is really unhealthy—not just for individuals, but for society. Because, again, all we have between us and the total breakdown of civilization is a series of successful conversations. If we can't reason with one another, there is no path forward, other than violence. Conversation or violence.[5]

It's true. Social media is driving us crazy, both individually and as a culture. Platforms like Facebook and Twitter have become lions' dens of cruelty and personal destruction.

Sam Harris doesn't believe in God, and he doesn't believe in Satan. But you and I, as Bible-believing Christians, know that Satan's influence on the world is real and pervasive. Satan is the god of this age—and Satan is the god of social media.

Should we shun Facebook and Twitter—have nothing to do with them because Satan is using these platforms for destructive purposes? No. There is hardly a human institution in existence that Satan does not exploit for his own ends.

Our public schools and universities have become enemy-held territories. Our news media and entertainment media are enemy-held territories. Our government has become an enemy-held territory. And yes, social media is enemy-held territory. That doesn't mean we surrender the schools, the media, the government, and social media to the enemy. It means we must invade these enemy-held territories and plant the banner of Christ on those territories.

What I'm suggesting is a risky proposition. As Sam Harris has suggested, social media is a bad neighborhood where cruel and angry people hang out. The cancel culture is alive and well on social media. Wherever Satan rules, there is danger—and Satan rules social media. As the apostle Peter reminds us, "Be alert and of sober mind. Your enemy the devil prowls around like a roaring lion looking for someone to devour" (1 Pet. 5:8).

Becoming a gladiator for the Lord on social media is not for everybody. If you decide to witness publicly for Christ on social media, you can expect to be hated, attacked, mocked, and persecuted. Before you venture into that lawless region of the internet, you need to make sure God has called you for that mission. You need to make sure the Holy Spirit has gifted you for that purpose. You need to make sure you have put on the whole armor of God so that you can withstand the fiery darts of the enemy. You need to make sure you have a heart full of God's love for ungodly people and a deep desire to lead them to Christ.

I'm not merely suggesting that you share a Christian

meme or retweet a Bible verse—though memes and verses can undoubtedly have an impact for Christ. I'm suggesting that God might be calling you to engage with non-Christians on social media the same way the apostle Paul engaged with the Greek philosophers on Mars Hill in Athens in Acts 17. I'm suggesting that God might be able to use your witness and your spiritual gifts to change minds and hearts on social media.

I want to caution you: If you tend to argue bitterly and respond angrily, if you have a desire to "own the atheists" and "put them in their place," then you should stay away from social media. You'll do more harm than good for the kingdom of God.

> Becoming a gladiator for the Lord on social media is not for everybody. If you decide to witness publicly for Christ on social media, you can expect to be hated, attacked, mocked, and persecuted.

But if you can be patient and kind when people insult you and mistreat you, if you can communicate the love and humility of Jesus even amid conflict and disagreement—then the Lord may be calling you to be His ambassador via the internet. If you are sure of God's calling, then go into battle confidently and fearlessly. Remember, Jesus knocked Satan's teeth out at the cross. Satan cannot bite or devour the believer—but he can still create a lot of havoc with his roar. Our adversary is working through people who hate Christ, but God still works through believers like you to love these enemies of Christ into His kingdom.

Speaking God's Truth to
a Post-Truth World

If you engage in conversations with unbelievers on social media or your campus or in your workplace or over the back fence, you may find that people often use unfair debating tactics. One of those tactics involves getting you to agree to a modest and noncontroversial statement. Then, once you have agreed to that statement, they advance a related statement that is utterly wrong. The goal of this tactic is to trap you into agreeing with utterly indefensible views.

For example, the arguer may say, "You and I agree that God is love. It says so right in your Bible, correct?" And that's true, of course. (See 1 John 4:8.) Once the arguer gets you to agree to the noncontroversial statement, he or she will go on to say something like, "And of course a loving God would never allow anyone to spend eternity in hell."

Or, "A loving God would never allow the kind of suffering we see in the world; therefore, God does not exist."

Or, "A loving God would not object to people loving each other any way they choose."

Or, "A loving God would never say that Jesus is the only way of salvation. A loving God would allow Himself to be found in every religion."

People will try to pull you off your message (the good news of Jesus Christ) and drag you into worldly political arguments. But as Jesus told Pontius Pilate, His kingdom is not of this world. His kingdom is not political. Our gospel is a message of salvation by grace through faith in Jesus Christ—not salvation through a political movement or social agenda.

When you share the good news with others, whether in person or on social media, don't let people maneuver you into pointless debates. They will try to get you to defend this politician or that policy or some historical event. They will try to set the rules of the discussion and maneuver you into debating by their rules. Don't let them box you in. Think outside their box. Keep bringing the conversation back to Jesus Christ and His love.

For example, an arguer might say, "How can any thinking person believe in Christianity? Look at all the hypocrites in the church."

You respond: "Yes, there are hypocrites in the church. Jesus predicted it would be this way. In Matthew 13, He tells a story called 'The Wheat and the Weeds.' He compares the church to a field of wheat. An enemy comes in and plants weeds among the wheat. The enemy is Satan, and the weeds are hypocrites—false Christians. You claim that hypocrites in the church disprove Christianity. No, hypocrites in the church merely verify that the words of Jesus are reliable and true."

You must know the Bible. You must have God's Word implanted in your heart and mind. As the apostle Peter tells us, "But in your hearts revere Christ as Lord. Always be prepared to give an answer to everyone who asks you to give the reason for the hope that you have. But do this with gentleness and respect" (1 Pet. 3:15).

Some people are honest inquirers after truth. Others simply want to win arguments and make others appear foolish. If you always answer gently and respectfully, if you support your beliefs with logic and Scripture, God can use that conversation to change hearts and minds.

If God has called you to speak His truth to a post-truth world through social media or over the back fence, if He is sending you on a mission to claim that enemy-held territory for Christ, then prepare yourself mentally and spiritually. Bathe your mind in His Word. Put on the full armor of God. Be ready to give an answer for the hope you have in Christ. Then live the adventure of faith!

The Message That Shapes History

The evidence shows that the Christian worldview made modern science and technology possible. The great scientists of the past were all committed Christians. They trusted the words God spoke through the psalmist.

> The heavens declare the glory of God; the skies proclaim the work of his hands. Day after day they pour forth speech; night after night they reveal knowledge.
> —Psalm 19:1–2

Believing that a rational God had created an orderly universe, they listened for the speech and the knowledge that the universe revealed. They searched for the physical and mathematical laws by which God had fashioned the universe—and they *found* those laws.

A German astronomer named Johannes Kepler believed that God was the Great Mathematician—and out of that conviction, Kepler discovered the laws that govern the motion of the planets. An English mathematician, Sir Isaac Newton, viewed God as the Great Engineer—and his Christian faith motivated him to delve into the laws of gravitation and motion, laying the foundation for modern engineering. An English physicist, Michael Faraday, saw God as the Great Physicist. His confidence in the orderliness of God's creation led him to profound discoveries in electricity and electromagnetism. Faraday even turned down an offer of knighthood from Queen Victoria, humbly remarking that the Lord Jesus would want him to remain "plain Mr. Faraday to the end."[6]

The Christian gospel has not only promoted the advancement of science but has also accelerated the progress of real social justice in the world. Bible-believing Christians led the movement that ended the slave trade in England and the abolition of slavery during the Second Great Awakening in America. Bible-believing Christians, led by Dr. Martin Luther King Jr., led the civil rights movement that desegregated America.

Evangelist Billy Graham also played a role in desegregation by inviting Dr. King to speak at a 1957 crusade. Graham insisted that crowds at his Southern crusades be integrated. When local officials put up ropes to divide the white and black sections, Graham would personally walk through the arena and tear the dividers down. Graham biographer Steven P. Miller said that Graham "contributed to the theological defeat of segregation."[7]

The gospel is still the message that shapes history and inspires positive change. In this unprecedented era of social distancing, social injustice, and social upheaval, the gospel of Jesus Christ is still the one prescription that can heal our society. You and I possess the only hope for our dangerously troubled world. That hope is the message of salvation by grace through faith in Jesus Christ alone.

The Lord called us to be "salt and light" in a corrupt and dark world. He has called us to proclaim His truth boldly in a world full of deception. You and I must accept the challenge of our times and offer this hope to a world that has lost all hope.

The troubled times in which we live did not catch God off guard. He knew these dark days were coming, and He positioned us here, at the crossroads of history, to shine His light into the darkness. As Paul wrote to the Christians at Philippi, "Whatever happens, conduct yourselves in a manner worthy of the gospel of Christ. Then, whether I come and see you or only hear about you in my absence, I will know that you stand firm in the one Spirit, striving together as one for the faith of the gospel" (Phil. 1:27).

We live in an age of apostasy when many people who have led evangelical churches and written evangelical books now disavow the faith of the gospel. They call themselves progressive Christians or emerging Christians or post-evangelical Christians. Still, they are the people Paul warned Timothy against—people who have "a form of godliness but denying its power. Have nothing to do with such people" (2 Tim. 3:5).

So I urge you: Stand firm! Don't be moved away from the faith of the gospel.

In Proverbs 22:28, God warns the people, "Do not move an ancient boundary stone set up by your ancestors." We endanger our society when we remove the landmarks laid down by our forefathers. This warning applies to the church as well as society. When progressive Christians start moving the boundaries of our faith—when they decide we can do away with the virgin birth, the death and resurrection of Jesus, or the entire Old Testament—and replace those boundaries with a "social gospel" of political activism, they are displaying a form of godliness while denying the power of the gospel.

We cannot change the world unless we first change ourselves. We must restore the boundaries and landmarks of our faith. The church has nothing to offer the world until we experience revival. The gospel transforms society by transforming one life at a time—beginning with your life and mine. As the gospel spreads virally throughout our society, we'll see a shockwave of God's healing love rippling across our world through the power of the Holy Spirit.

There is only one solution to this present crisis: we must repent of our sins and experience the revival that flows from God's redemption. Every spiritual awakening throughout history began with the repentance of God's people. The most urgent response to our present crisis is a personal and individual response.

Revival begins with me. And revival begins with you.

A Role Model for Us All

Gail Blair is a retired nurse in her early sixties, living in the town of Westerly, Rhode Island. She was forced to retire from nursing in 1991 when she was diagnosed with a vision disorder that eventually left her blind. Even though she could no longer work with patients in a hospital, she wanted to serve God and spread the good news of the gospel.

She contacted the Pocket Testament League, and they supplied her with copies of the Gospel of John and gave her advice on how to approach people in a public park and offer the gospel booklets.

So Gail Blair began visiting Wilcox Park, a short walk from her home. Following the Pocket Testament League's advice, she would offer a Gospel of John—no pressure, no pestering, no arguing. Sometimes, people would engage her in conversation, and she would have a chance to share her faith with them.

She was lawfully exercising her First Amendment freedom. But in June 2019, somebody complained.

Officials of the Memorial and Library Association, which had oversight of the Westerly Library and Wilcox Park, called the police, telling them that Gail Blair was stopping park visitors and giving them religious pamphlets. It's hard to picture a blind woman in her sixties physically stopping people in the park and forcing religious pamphlets into their hands against their will.

And consider this paradox: In the early 1990s, federal courts ruled that panhandling—aggressively begging for money in public places—was constitutionally protected speech. Nowhere does the First Amendment specifically mention panhandling. Yet the rights to free speech and free exercise of religion are spelled out in black and white in the First Amendment—and those rights were denied to Gail Blair. Unfortunately, many people in positions of authority have a backward view of the First Amendment.

The police officers, acting on the complaint from the Association, approached Gail Blair and told her she was banned from the park and the adjacent library. She could not return to the park for two years.

The following month, Gail Blair's church held a vacation Bible school event at Wilcox Park. She volunteered to help. She wasn't handing out the Gospel of John to strangers. She was simply assisting with activities for the children.

The police showed up and told her she was trespassing. They made her leave and warned her that if she returned to the park, she would be arrested and jailed.

In June 2020, Blair's attorneys filed a discrimination complaint with the Rhode Island Commission for Human Rights.[8] The case is still pending as I write these words. I don't know how the commission will decide Gail Blair's case—and that's not the point of the story. The point is this: Gail Blair is a role model for you and me. She is courageously exercising her rights under the Constitution to share the gospel and expand the kingdom of God. She doesn't let blindness stop her; neither does she allow the park officials and police to stop her. God has given her a mission. He has sent her into enemy-held territory—Wilcox Park in Westerly, Rhode Island—with orders to plant the flag of King Jesus on that ground.

In effect, Gail Blair is saying to those park officials, "I must obey God rather than human beings." She is one of the latest in a long line of courageous witnesses for Christ—a spiritual lineage stretching back to the apostle Peter.

So we have to ask ourselves: What are we risking for Christ today? How have we helped spread the good news of Jesus Christ during this present crisis? How are we making a difference in the world through our witness for Him? What enemy-held territory has God staked out for us to conquer in His name?

There's no time for hesitation. The world is collapsing all around us.

Let's pray. Let's put on our armor.

Let's conquer.

EPILOGUE

GOD'S SEVEN-STEP SOLUTION

NAVY CHAPLAIN HOWELL Forgy was stationed aboard the cruiser USS *New Orleans* during the surprise attack on Pearl Harbor, Sunday morning, December 7, 1941. As enemy planes screamed overhead, the antiaircraft guns of the *New Orleans* were silent. The antiaircraft gunners had no ammunition. The ship's only defense consisted of sailors on the deck, firing frantically at the planes with rifles and pistols.

Chaplain Forgy and some other crewmen hurried down to the ordnance storeroom to retrieve the ammunition. To their dismay, they found the storeroom locked—the crewman with the keys was away on shore leave. They succeeded in breaking the lock and opening the storeroom, but the electric ammunition hoist had no power and was unusable.

So Chaplain Forgy and the other crewmen formed a human chain—a "bucket brigade"—to pass the shells from man to man up to the deck. Soon antiaircraft guns began firing, defending the *New Orleans* from the enemy planes. The shells were heavy, and the work was exhausting. Chaplain Forgy could feel the strain in his muscles, and he saw that some of his fellow crewmen were growing weary.

He reached out and clapped the next man on the back and shouted, "Praise the Lord and pass the ammunition!"[1]

Crewmen later recalled that Chaplain Forgy's words renewed their strength. The antiaircraft gunners fended off the attacking planes, and the *New Orleans* suffered only minor damage from a single fragmentation bomb. The ship went on to serve in the battles at the Coral Sea, Midway, and the Eastern Solomon Islands.[2]

Today a new crisis is upon us. We are at war, engaged in a life-or-death struggle called spiritual warfare. Our enemy is merciless and deadly. The church is a "bucket brigade" of warriors whom God has called to take the fight to the enemy. But many Christians have grown weary. Many are spiritually exhausted. We need to encourage each other to "praise the Lord and pass the ammunition." And we need to experience the encouragement of God, clapping us on the back and renewing our strength.

As the influence of the Christian church has declined throughout society, we are witnessing a loss of respect for the truth, human life, the family, and God. Our world is splintering into hostile tribes and warring factions, fueled by hate and cruelty on the internet. Although foreign nations and terror groups are trying to do us harm, the *real* threat to our civilization comes from among us—a steep decline of faith, truth, and morality, weakening our society from within.

In a time of crisis, we need all hands on deck. We need Christians who will leap into action, do the job that needs to be done, and rally their fellows with words of encouragement and inspiration. Even in this crisis, there is hope—but only if God's people wake up in time and report for duty.

What can one Christian, one family, or one church do? Let me share with you God's seven-step solution to our present crisis. Armed with God's truth and armored for the spiritual battle ahead, you can help change the world. It all begins with the life-changing, world-changing good news of Jesus Christ.

So here are God's seven steps to solving this present crisis, with each step broken down into essential principles.

Step One: Remember the Truth

1. *Stand firm on the truth of the gospel.* Jesus is the way, the truth, and the life—no one comes to the Father except through Him. We must never be ashamed of sharing the gospel with others. We must never pollute the pure Christian gospel with false teachings from other religions. We reject the temptation to water down the gospel to win friendship with this dying world.

2. *Reject racism and bigotry in all its forms.* In Christ there is neither Jew nor Gentile, neither slave nor free, neither male nor female, for we are all one in Christ Jesus.

3. *Remember the Great Commandment.* In Matthew 22:37–38, Jesus says, "'Love the Lord your God with all your heart and with all your soul and with all your mind.' This is the first and greatest commandment." The heart is the seat of the emotions. The soul is the seat of the will. The mind is the seat of the intellect. We are to love God not only with emotions of adoration and

an obedient will but also with our intellect, our love of truth. Our faith is based on a foundation of truth and irrefutable evidence.

4. *Keep your rational mind in charge of your emotions.* Remember the words of my late friend, John R. W. Stott: "The mind should be the thermostat which sets the temperature for the emotions."

5. *Stay salty!* Jesus said, "You are the salt of the earth. But if the salt loses its saltiness, how can it be made salty again? It is no longer good for anything, except to be thrown out and trampled underfoot" (Matt. 5:13). Share the savory salt of the gospel wherever you go.

Step Two: Restore the Soul

1. *Seek God's approval, not the approval of other people.* If you abandon the foundational truths of Christianity, the world will love you. Simply agree with the world that Jesus is *a* way to God—not *the* way; dismiss the Bible as nothing but a book of fables; adopt the secular political agenda of the culture and call it "Christianity"—that's a surefire formula for winning friends in the world.

But if you seek friendship with the world, you won't be a friend of God. If we are not at odds with the culture, we are at odds with God.

2. *Be on guard against false teachings.* Jesus warned, "Watch out for false prophets. They come to you in sheep's clothing, but inwardly they are ferocious wolves" (Matt. 7:15). Satan has sent his false teachers into the evangelical church. They may sound like sheep, but they seek to tear down the church from within. Don't be

fooled by wolves disguised as sheep. Test every teaching, every doctrine, against the Word of God.

3. *Make decisions on the basis of God's truth.* Search the Scriptures and pray before you buy a car or home, accept a job offer, choose a college, or make a business deal. Are you honoring God with your spending, savings, debt, and giving to God? Does your voting reflect biblical truth and values? Does God want you to date that person? Does He approve of the way you spend your free time—the movies and TV shows you stream, the time you spend on the internet, the time you spend on your phone, or the company you keep? Every action we take and every decision we make should be based on God's truth.

> **If we are not at odds with the culture, we are at odds with God.**

4. *Don't fear the world and its persecution.* Don't be ashamed of the gospel. If God prompts you to speak His truth or challenge falsehood, take a moment to pray— then speak up! Proverbs 29:25 tells us, "Fear of man will prove to be a snare, but whoever trusts in the LORD is kept safe." Don't let Satan ensnare you with fear—trust God, speak boldly, act boldly, and vanquish your fears through faith and obedience.

5. *Don't be afraid.* Even though we walk through the valley of the shadow of death, we do not fear the evil of this world. Jesus, the Good Shepherd, is with us, comforting us, providing for us, and guarding us. He restores our souls and leads us into paths of true righteousness. Amid threats and persecution, He anoints our heads with oil and fills our cups with overflowing

blessings. Memorize the twenty-third Psalm and repeat it often—especially in times of fear.

6. *Remember your eternal destiny.* We were made for heaven. What a tragedy it is that we so easily lose sight of our heavenly destiny. God has promised that we will have glorified, resurrection bodies—just like the resurrected body of Jesus. Paul tells us that Jesus "will transform our lowly bodies so that they will be like his glorious body" (Phil. 3:21). We'll live on a new Earth, which God promised to us in the Old and New Testaments. Heaven is an objective reality. Whenever opposition and persecution come your way, stay focused on your eternal destiny.

Step Three: Revitalize the Family

1. *Protect your children from the horrors of the internet.* Every internet-connected device—including a smart-phone—is a doorway to a world of horrifying images that a child might never unsee. And it's not enough to protect your child from the devices under your control.

I recently heard about a young boy who came home from school, crying uncontrollably. It took the child's father more than an hour to get the boy to talk about why he was crying. It turned out that a friend at school had shown him an internet website with disturbing images. The boy wouldn't say what kind of images, but he was afraid to go to sleep for weeks afterward.

The threat to your child from the World Wide Web grows greater every day. Don't leave your child's soul unguarded. Have a conversation (or a series of conversations) with your children about the dangers of the internet. Set firm rules about what they are permitted to watch on internet-connected screens—including the screens in the hands of their classmates. Prepare them to withstand peer pressure, dares, and taunts from kids who may want your children to see things that could scar them for life.

2. *Know who your children's friends are.* Who are they calling? Who are they texting? How are they being influenced? Remember the biblical warning, "Bad company corrupts good character" (1 Cor. 15:33).

3. *Pray for your children.* Pray for God's protection over their minds, hearts, and souls. Pray that they flee temptation—and that they confess their sins and receive God's forgiveness when they fail. Ask your kids daily what they would like you to pray for, then pray for their requests throughout the day. Keep a notebook of prayer requests, and mark the date that God answered those prayers.

4. *Pray with your children.* Make prayer a regular part of your family life. Sit down with your preschooler, and thank God for a beautiful day or a delicious snack. Pray with elementary-grade children for their teachers, their friends, their needs, and their concerns. Pray with teens about their pressures and temptations and difficulties at school. As you pray, thank God for His everlasting love. (See Psalm 103:17.) Ask God to fill your family with joy, peace, and blessing. (See Romans 15:13.)

5. *Help your children memorize Scripture.* Make God's Word the focus of your family life. Help your children to feed on Scripture from their earliest years.

6. *Build moral and spiritual guardrails around your private behavior, your marriage relationship, and your home.* If you struggle with lust or addiction, talk to a

Christian counselor. Ask trusted friends to hold you accountable. Do whatever it takes to guard against temptation. Remember the example of King David. Even a single unguarded moment of lust can lead to grievous consequences and a ruined reputation.

7. *Make sure that God is at the center of your family.* There should be no separation of your family into "sacred" and "secular" compartments. A vibrant, dynamic relationship with God should permeate every corner of your home, every aspect of your family life. Godly children come from godly families.

If yours is a blended family, your children may spend a significant amount of time in a family structure with a different set of rules, and even a different faith tradition or no faith instruction at all. When your children return to your family, you may feel you have to undo a lot of damage that was done in the other family. Even though such situations are less than ideal, keep praying with your children. Keep teaching them the principles of God's Word. Persevere in keeping God at the center of your family. Avoid criticizing the other parent and the other home.

It's not easy raising children in blended families, but if you stay focused on God and His love, He will give you the strength and wisdom to raise your children to know Him and love Him throughout their lives.

Step Four: Reestablish the Classroom

1. *Support conscientious, caring public school teachers.* Pray for them. Volunteer to help them. Encourage them

and let them know that you appreciate their hard work and dedication.

2. *Get involved and be aware of what your children are being taught.* Like those two Indiana moms in chapter 4, you may be surprised by the curriculum in your children's public or private school. Join your local parent-teacher organization, attend school board meetings, do your homework, and be informed. If need be, become an activist on behalf of your children's education.

3. *Encourage your children to be witnesses for Jesus at school.* They have a First Amendment right to share their faith, to write papers about God, to wear Christian symbols, and so forth. Most teachers and school administrators understand the First Amendment—but some have bought into secular-left, anti-Christian propaganda. Know the Constitution, know your rights, and know your child's rights. Pray for boldness and take a stand for God's truth at your child's school.

4. *Tune in to what your children are learning at school.* At dinnertime, engage them in conversations about their day and their school subjects. Ask questions and listen attentively to everything they say.

5. *If the public school doesn't offer your child a good education, consider a private Christian school or homeschooling.* Parents who homeschool or pay for private schooling make enormous sacrifices. Homeschooling is harder than it looks. But if you are committed to giving your children a high-quality education at home, and protecting them from worldly indoctrination, you just might give them a significant advantage in life.

6. *Pray for your children before, during, and after school.* Go into your children's bedrooms while they

are in school and pray for them. Ask God to watch over them physically, mentally, emotionally, and spiritually. Ask Him to safeguard your children from the destructive influence of Satan and this fallen world.

Step Five: Respect Our Freedoms

1. *Know your rights.* An excellent place to start is with the Bill of Rights, the first ten amendments to the Constitution. Learn about the history of the Declaration of Independence and the Constitution. If a university official says you can't talk about God on campus, or if a city official says you can't hand out gospel literature at the park, respectfully assert your constitutional rights. Make sure you clearly understand your rights and that you know what the Constitution does and does not protect.

2. *Defend the rights of others.* If you see that someone has been unfairly attacked or silenced, speak up for that person. Speak out against injustice.

3. *Pray for boldness—and discernment.* There is a time to speak out and a time to hold your peace. If you feel God calling you to speak boldly in defense of His truth, pray for courage and wisdom. Then speak the words He gives you to speak.

Always listen for the leading of the Spirit. There may be times when the Lord tells you, "Say nothing to this person—his heart is hardened against the gospel, and he would only do you harm." Jesus put it this way in the Sermon on the Mount: "Do not give dogs what is sacred; do not throw your pearls to pigs. If you do, they may trample them under their feet, and turn and tear you to pieces" (Matt. 7:6).

4. *Consider a career in the media.* Are you a young person wondering if God is calling you into the news or entertainment media? God undoubtedly wants courageous young Christians to take that enemy-held territory in His name. But be aware that many media companies have become lions' dens for Christians. If you can't withstand the pressure to conform, you may be eaten alive. Make sure you are spiritually strong and have a network of committed prayer warriors in your corner.

5. *Pray for young Christians in the media.* If you are a parent, teacher, youth leader, or pastor, and you know young people who are in media, be an influential mentor to them. Cover them in prayer—they'll need it. Support them as they seek to become salt and light in an increasingly dark and corrosive industry.

Step Six: Reform Our Society

1. *Morally and spiritually purify yourself.* Repent of your sins and turn to God for forgiveness and restoration.

After King Solomon completed construction of the great temple in Jerusalem, the Lord spoke to him and said, "When I shut up the heavens so that there is no rain, or command locusts to devour the land or send a plague among my people, if my people, who are called by my name, will humble themselves and pray and seek my face and turn from their wicked ways, then I will hear from heaven, and I will forgive their sin and will heal their land. Now my eyes will be open and my ears attentive to the prayers offered in this place" (2 Chron. 7:13–15).

And the psalmist said, "Blessed is the nation whose God is the LORD, the people he chose for his inheritance" (Ps. 33:12). We can't expect God to bless us if we are continuing in sin and disobedience. Seek God's face—and ask Him to heal our land.

2. *Pray for our nation.* Thank God for our country and ask Him to send revival. Ask Him to turn every church and home into a house of prayer. Ask Him to purify His people so that the bride of Christ would be faithful and holy. Ask Him to set us apart as His followers, consecrated to His service and the preaching of His gospel.

3. *Persevere in sharing the gospel with everyone around you.* Whether people receive the good news with joy or reject it, never give up. Never stop witnessing.

One of the most comforting and sobering books of the Bible for troubled times is the Book of Jeremiah. It's the story of a man who spent forty years preaching a message of repentance and judgment to the nation of Judah. His preaching fell on deaf ears. Throughout those four decades of prophetic ministry, Jeremiah didn't see a single person—not one!—come to repentance and salvation.

God, speaking through Jeremiah, told the nation of Judah, "If at any time I announce that a nation or kingdom is to be uprooted, torn down and destroyed, and if that nation I warned repents of its evil, then I will relent and not inflict on it the disaster I had planned. And if at another time I announce that a nation or kingdom is to be built up and planted, and if it does evil in my sight and does not obey me, then I will reconsider the good I had intended to do for it" (Jer. 18:7–10).

You and I have inherited the message of Jeremiah, and we must spread this message to our nation. We must call our fellow citizens to repentance. Like Jeremiah, we may not see anyone respond to the gospel. God is responsible for the results, not us. The Holy Spirit moves people to repentance, not us. Our only responsibility is to be faithful in speaking out and praying for our nation.

As Paul told Timothy, "I urge, then, first of all, that petitions, prayers, intercession and thanksgiving be made for all people—for kings and all those in authority, that we may live peaceful and quiet lives in all godliness and holiness. This is good, and pleases God our Savior, who wants all people to be saved and to come to a knowledge of the truth" (1 Tim. 2:1–4). Let's pray together for our nation—earnestly, continually, with broken hearts and tear-filled eyes.

Step Seven: Revive the Church

1. *Demonstrate the forgiving love of Jesus at all times.* These are times of trial and testing for the church. We are ringed about by enemies who hate God and His church. Let's respond to their hate with the love of Jesus. Let's respond with prayer, compassion, and forgiveness.

2. *Put on the full armor of God.* Prepare for spiritual warfare—and remember that your enemy is not flesh and blood. Your enemy is Satan and his demons.

Put on the belt of God's truth, the breastplate of His righteousness, and protect your feet with the gospel of peace. Take up the shield of faith that will fend off the flaming arrows of Satan, guard your thoughts with the helmet of your salvation, and arm yourself with the sword of the Spirit, God's Word.

3. *Know* what *you believe and* why *you believe.* Study the Scriptures. Learn how to explain to others why you believe the Bible is God's revealed truth, why you believe in the historical reality of the resurrection, and why you are confident of your eternal life.

> The Holy Spirit moves people to repentance, not us. Our only responsibility is to be faithful in speaking out and praying for our nation.

4. *Pray for opportunities to exercise your spiritual gifts.* Every believer has spiritual gifts, and every believer must report for duty. God has a mission for you. He might be calling you to volunteer in your church or to spread the good news in your neighborhood or on your campus, or He might send you to the far corners of the earth in His name. Pray that He would reveal His calling to you in an unmistakable way. Tell Him, "Here I am, Lord. Send me."

5. *Encourage your pastors and teachers.* Pray for them, and send them notes and emails of appreciation and affirmation. Tell them how their ministry has impacted your life. Encourage them to continue preaching the uncompromised Word of God with boldness and power.

Blood for Enemies

Charles Colson told of an incident that took place in northern Iraq when that nation was torn by terrorism and war. Two Iraqi insurgents were placing a roadside bomb, intending to kill American soldiers, when they were fired on by a US Army helicopter. The insurgents were severely wounded but alive. Medevac helicopters flew the injured men to an army hospital at Camp Speicher, near Tikrit.

Because of his extensive wounds and massive bleeding, one of the insurgents needed thirty pints of blood. (The human body typically holds about ten pints, so the equivalent of his entire bloodstream would have to be replaced three times while surgeons tried to stop the bleeding.) The hospital was low on blood because of recent attacks that left many soldiers wounded. So the doctors called for volunteer donors. Within minutes, a line of American soldiers formed, all ready to give blood to the enemy. A reporter went to the first soldier in line and asked why he was willing to give blood to an enemy insurgent.

The soldier replied, "A human life is a human life." Reflecting on this response, Colson wrote:

> I have never seen a more dramatic example of worldviews in contrast, nor have I been prouder of an American G.I. On one hand, we have the horrors of a civilization that values death—even the death of its own children—if by killing them they can hurt the infidels. On the other side, we have a story that makes us realize just how deeply embedded within American life is our Judeo-Christian heritage. This heritage teaches that human life is sacred—even the life of an enemy who falls into our hands.[3]

We follow the One who gave His blood for His enemies. You and I were once His enemies, but because of the cross on which He died, Jesus now calls us His friends.

Let's rejoice that we live in these exciting days. Let's celebrate that God is going to do an amazing work before our eyes. In this present crisis, the world seems to have gone mad. But we follow the One who restores our sanity, who heals our diseases, who forgives our sin, who raises us from death to life.

As followers of Jesus, we are ready to lay down our lives and give our blood to turn God's enemies into friends. Jesus is the solution to our present crisis.

Let us purify our hearts and enthrone Him as our King.

NOTES

Introduction

1. Jonathan Grant et al., "Population Implosion? Low Fertility and Policy Responses in the European Union," Rand Corporation, accessed July 27, 2020, https://www.rand.org/pubs/research_briefs/RB9126.html.
2. David M. Walker, *Comeback America: Turning the Country Around and Restoring Fiscal Responsibility* (New York: Random House, 2009), 36–37.
3. Niall Ferguson, "America, the Fragile Empire," *Dallas Morning News*, March 19, 2010, https://www.dallasnews.com/opinion/commentary/2010/03/19/niall-ferguson-america-the-fragile-empire/.
4. Charles Krauthammer, "Decline Is a Choice," *Washington Examiner*, October 19, 2009, https://www.washingtonexaminer.com/weekly-standard/decline-is-a-choice-270813.

Chapter 1

1. "Baylor Disputes Student Group's Claim That Kaitlin Curtice Prayed to 'Mother Mystery' at Chapel," *Relevant*, February 18, 2020, embedded video accessed March 1, 2020, https://relevantmagazine.com/current/baylor-disputes-student-groups-claim-that-kaitlin-curtice-prayed-to-mother-mystery-at-chapel/. (Note: The video accessed and transcribed by the author at that site is no longer available; a notice reads: "Sorry. Because of its privacy settings, this video cannot be played here." Author has been unable to find another internet location where the video is still posted. However, quoted material was transcribed verbatim from an audio recording made before the video was removed from the site.); https://relevantmagazine.com/god/some-baylor-students-are-upset-over-kaitlin-curtices-chapel-prayer/.

2. Emily McFarlan Miller, "Potawatomi Christian Chapel Speaker Kaitlin Curtice Draws Ire of Baylor Student Group," Religion News Service, February 20, 2020, https://religionnews.com/2020/02/20/potawatomi-christian-chapel-speaker-kaitlin-curtice-draws-ire-of-baylor-student-group/.

3. Michael Youssef, "No, We Will Not Let Our Christian Colleges Become 'Woke,'" *Christian Post*, March 10, 2020, https://static.christianpost.com/voices/no-we-will-not-let-our-christian-colleges-become-woke.html.

4. Miller, "Potawatomi Christian Chapel Speaker Kaitlin Curtice Draws Ire of Baylor Student Group."

5. Kaitlin Curtice, "The Sacredness of the Earth as She Is," *Sojourners*, August 12, 2019, https://sojo.net/articles/sacredness-earth-she.

6. Youssef, "No, We Will Not Let Our Christian Colleges Become 'Woke.'"

7. John 8:31–32, 36.

8. H. S. Thayer, ed., *Newton's Philosophy of Nature: Selections from His Writings* (Mineola, NY: Dover, 2005), 42.

9. America's Founding Documents, "Declaration of Independence: A Transcription," National Archives, accessed November 19, 2019, https://www.archives.gov/founding-docs/declaration-transcript.

10. Richard Corliss, "Cinema: Our Critic Rides a Time Machine," *Time*, February 10, 1997, http://content.time.com/time/magazine/article/0,9171,985897,00.html.

11. Lynn Rasmussen, *Men are Easy, A Simple Guide to Fun, Sexy, Happy, and Easy Relationships* (Makwao, Maui, HI: Mohala Media, LLC., 2007), 33.

12. Jason Slotkin, "U.K. Cellphone Towers Ablaze As Conspiracy Theories Link 5G Networks To COVID-19," NPR, April 4, 2020, https://www.npr.org/sections/coronavirus-live-updates/2020/04/04/827343675/u-k-cellphone-towers-ablaze-as-conspiracy-theories-link-5g-networks-to-covid-19; Lee Brown, "Woody Harrelson Among Stars Sharing Coronavirus Conspiracy Theories Tied to 5G," *New York Post*, April 5, 2020, https://nypost.

com/2020/04/05/woody-harrelson-sharing-coronavirus-conspiracy-theory-tied-to-5g/.

13. "Competing Worldviews Influence Today's Christians: Research Releases in Culture & Media," Barna, May 9, 2017, https://www.barna.com/research/competing-worldviews-influence-todays-christians/.
14. "Competing Worldviews Influence Today's Christians."
15. "Competing Worldviews Influence Today's Christians."
16. Author uncredited, "John F. Kennedy Jr & Carolyn Bessette-Kennedy: How Did They Die?," Heavy, July 12, 2019, https://heavy.com/news/2019/07/john-f-kennedy-jr-death-die-how/.

Chapter 2

1. TP Interviews, "The Think Piece Interview: John Shelby Spong," Think Piece, October 14, 2013, https://thinkpiecepublishing.com/interviews/the-think-piece-interview-bishop-john-shelby-spong/.
2. Brandon Withrow, "They Have Faith Their Church Will Change," *Daily Beast*, updated April 13, 2017, https://www.thedailybeast.com/they-have-faith-their-church-will-change.
3. Brian McLaren, "A Tale of Two Gospels," Slideshare.net, slide 43; www.slideshare.net/brianmclaren/leading-in-tradition-2017091.
4. C. S. Lewis, *Mere Christianity* (New York: HarperOne, 2001), 134.
5. Alice Su, "A Doctor Was Arrested for Warning China about the Coronavirus. Then He Died of It," *Los Angeles Times*, February 6, 2020, https://www.latimes.com/world-nation/story/2020-02-06/coronavirus-china-xi-li-wenliang; Bernardo Cervellera, "Wuhan Public Security Bureau Apologizes to Li Wenliang's Family over 'Inappropriate Reprimand,'" AsiaNews.it, March 20, 2020, http://www.asianews.it/news-en/Wuhan-Public-Security-Bureau-apologises-to-Li-Wenliang's-family-over-'inappropriate-reprimand'-49616.html.

Chapter 3

1. Pat Williams, *Souls of Steel: How to Build Character in Ourselves and Our Kids* (Nashville: FaithWords, 2008), 50–51.
2. Bill Swainson, ed., *Encarta Book of Quotations* (New York: St. Martin's Press, 2000), 303, https://books.google.com.
3. Patrick Fagan, "The Real Root Causes of Violent Crime: The Breakdown of Marriage, Family, and Community," The Heritage Foundation, March 17, 1995, https://www.heritage.org/crime-and-justice/report/the-real-root-causes-violent-crime-the-breakdown-marriage-family-and.
4. Rodney Clapp, *A Peculiar People* (Downers Grove, IL: InterVaristy Press, 1996), 176.
5. Gil Reavill, *Smut: A Sex-Industry Insider (and Concerned Father) Says Enough Is Enough* (New York: Penguin, 2005), 24–25.
6. Reavill, *Smut*, 20.
7. Michael Reagan, *Twice Adopted* (Nashville: Broadman & Holman, 2004), 89–108.

Chapter 4

1. "School Officials Censor God from Graduation Speech," Liberty Institute, accessed July 29, 2020, https://www.libertyinstitute.org/hamby.
2. Katherine Weber, "10-Year-Old Banned From Writing About God By Memphis Teacher, Told to Remove Paper From School Property," *Christian Post*, September 12, 2013, https://www.christianpost.com/news/10-year-old-banned-from-writing-about-god-by-memphis-teacher-told-to-remove-paper-from-school-property.html.
3. David Limbaugh, *Persecution: How Liberals Are Waging War Against Christians* (Washington, DC: Regnery, 2003), 20.
4. Kat Eschner, "This Supreme Court Justice Was a KKK Member," *Smithsonian Magazine*, February 27, 2017, https://www.smithsonianmag.com/smart-news/supreme-court-justice-was-kkk-member-180962254/.

5. Pat Williams, *Extreme Dreams Depend on Teams* (Nashville: Hashette, 2009), 97.
6. "Bill Ayers," Discover the Networks, updated June 6, 2020, https://www.discoverthenetworks.org/individuals/bill-ayers.
7. "Common Core," Discover the Networks, updated June 2, 2020, https://www.discoverthenetworks.org/organizations/common-core/.
8. "Common Core States 2020," World Population Review, accessed July 29, 2020, https://worldpopulationreview.com/states/common-core-states/.
9. Maggie Gallagher, "Two Moms vs. Common Core," *National Review*, May 12, 2013, https://www.nationalreview.com/2013/05/two-moms-vs-common-core-maggie-gallagher/.
10. Gallagher, "Two Moms vs. Common Core."
11. Mary Jo Anderson, "Common Core Goes Global," *Crisis*, November 20, 2013, https://www.crisismagazine.com/2013/common-core-goes-global.
12. Mercedes K. Schneider, *A Chronicle of Echoes: Who's Who in the Implosion of American Public Education* (Charlotte, NC: Information Age Publishing, Inc, 2014), 170–171.
13. Schneider, *A Chronicle of Echoes*, 172.
14. Schneider, *A Chronicle of Echoes*, 172.
15. Schneider, *A Chronicle of Echoes*, 172.
16. Joy Pullmann, "9 Years Into Common Core, Test Scores Are Down, Indoctrination Up," *The Federalist*, November 5, 2018, https://thefederalist.com/2018/11/05/9-years-common-core-test-scores-indoctrination/.
17. UnboundEd, "The Intersection of Standards and Equity—Kate Gerson," transcription of YouTube video, November 30, 2018, https://www.youtube.com/watch?v=fl_IZkez1Ko.
18. Conor Friedersdorf, "Too Much Stigma, Not Enough Persuasion," *The Atlantic*, November 30, 2016, https://www.theatlantic.com/politics/archive/2016/11/the-scourge-of-the-left-too-much-stigma-not-enough-persuasion/508961/.

19. Lindsey Tepe, "States, Not Publishers, Driving Innovation in the Curriculum Marketplace," New America, November 2, 2017, https://www.newamerica. org/education-policy/edcentral/states-driving-curriculum-innovation/.

20. Sean Cavanagh, "Report Breaks Down the Big Appetite for EngageNY Among Nation's Teachers," EdWeek Market Brief, March 28, 2017, https://marketbrief. edweek.org/marketplace-k-12/report-breaks-big-appetite-engageny-among-nations-teachers/.

21. Ray Raphael, *A People's History of the American Revolution* (New York: The New Press, 2016), 23 [capitalization normalized for readability].

22. "Education: Boston Tea Party Was Act Of Terrorism? Texas Public Schools Teaching New History Lesson," Huffington Post, November 26, 2012, https://www.huffpost.com/entry/boston-tea-party-was-act-_n_2193916.

23. Adam Wright, "Lumberton High School Classroom Photo Sparks Controversy," Campus Watch, February 26, 2013, https://www.meforum.org/campus-watch/20597/lumberton-high-school-classroom-photo-sparks.

24. Randy DeSoto, "Big Gov't Leftists Will Be Furious: Poll Finds 40% of Families More Likely To Homeschool After Lockdowns," The Western Journal, May 21, 2020, https://www.westernjournal.com/big-govt-leftists-will-furious-poll-finds-40-families-likely-home-school-lockdowns/.

25. Michael Reagan, *The New Reagan Revolution: How Ronald Reagan's Principles Can Restore America's Greatness Today* (New York: Saint Martin's, 2010), 190.

26. Michael Smith, "Homeschooling: California Court Reverses Decision," *Washington Times*, September 7, 2008, http://washingtontimes.com/news/2008/sep/07/california-court-reverses-decision/.

27. Elizabeth Anderson, "Homeschooling Parents in California County Told that Homeschooling was Illegal," *Parent Herald*, July 28, 2008, http://

www.parentherald.com/articles/57534/20160728/
homeschooling-parents-california-county-
told-illegal.htm; Veronica Neffinger, "Right to
Homeschool Children under Attack in California,"
ChristianHeadlines.com, July 28, 2016, https://www.
christianheadlines.com/blog/right-to-homeschool-
children-under-attack-in-california.html.

28. Jonathan Keller, "Defeat of AB 2756: Huge Victory for
California Homeschoolers," California Family Council,
April 27, 2018, https://californiafamily.org/2018/defeat-
of-ab-2756-huge-victory-for-california-homeschoolers/.

29. Os Guinness, *American Hour* (New York: The Free
Press, 1993), 203.

30. Dr. Brian D. Ray, "Homeschool Progress Report 2009:
Academic Achievement and Demographics," ERIC
Institute of Education Sciences, 2009, https://files.eric.
ed.gov/fulltext/ED535134.pdf.

31. Erin O'Donnell, "The Risks of Homeschooling,"
Harvard Magazine, May–June 2020, https://www.
harvardmagazine.com/2020/05/right-now-risks-
homeschooling.

32. C. S. Lewis, *The Complete C. S. Lewis Signature
Classics* (New York: HarperOne, 2007), 293–294.

Chapter 5

1. "Press Briefing by Members of the President's
Coronavirus Task Force," The White House, January
31, 2020, https://www.whitehouse.gov/briefings-
statements/press-briefing-members-presidents-
coronavirus-task-force/.

2. America's Founding Documents, "The Bill of Rights:
A Transcription," National Archives, accessed July 29,
2020, https://www.archives.gov/founding-docs/bill-of-
rights-transcript.

3. "Gov. Kemp Updates Georgians on COVID-19,"
Governor Brian P. Kemp, April 20, 2020, https://gov.
georgia.gov/press-releases/2020-04-20/gov-kemp-
updates-georgians-covid-19.

4. Amanda Mull, "Georgia's Experiment in Human Sacrifice," *The Atlantic*, April 29, 2020, https://www.theatlantic.com/health/archive/2020/04/why-georgia-reopening-coronavirus-pandemic/610882/.
5. Jacqueline Howard, "Georgia's Daily Coronavirus Deaths Will Nearly Double by August With Relaxed Social Distancing, Model Suggests," CNN, April 28, 2020, https://www.cnn.com/2020/04/28/health/georgia-coronavirus-death-projections/index.html.
6. Willoughby Mariano, "Coronavirus Cases, Deaths Projected to Rise As Georgia Reopens," *Atlanta Journal and Constitution*, May 6, 2020, https://www.ajc.com/news/state--regional-govt--politics/cases-deaths-projected-rise-state-reopens/q4jJqCtX9bmqujkZPa5OdK/.
7. German Lopez, "Why Georgia's Reopening Hasn't Led to a Surge in Coronavirus Cases (So Far)," Vox, June 4, 2020, https://www.vox.com/2020/6/4/21267769/georgia-coronavirus-pandemic-covid-cases-deaths-data.
8. "George Floyd Death: Widespread Unrest as Curfews Defied Across US," BBC, May 31, 2020, https://www.bbc.com/news/world-us-canada-52865206.
9. Sara M. Moniuszko, "Chris Cuomo Calls for Police Accountability: 'Too Many See the Protests as the Problem,'" *USA Today*, June 3, 2020, https://www.usatoday.com/story/entertainment/celebrities/2020/06/03/chris-cuomo-calls-police-accountability-defends-protests/3133326001/.
10. Natalie Escobar, "One Author's Controversial View: 'In Defense of Looting,'" NPR, August 27, 2020, https://www.npr.org/sections/codeswitch/2020/08/27/906642178/one-authors-argument-in-defense-of-looting?t=1598683114434.
11. Escobar, "One Author's Controversial View: 'In Defense of Looting.'"
12. M. D. Kittle, "With Businesses Destroyed, Kenosha Owners Ponder Their Future," NationalInterest.org, September 7, 2020, https://nationalinterest.org/blog/reboot/

businesses-destroyed-kenosha-owners-ponder-their-future-168274.

13. Susannah Cullinane, "Retired St. Louis Police Captain Killed after Responding to a Pawnshop Alarm during Looting," CNN.com, August 27, 2020, https://www.cnn.com/2020/06/03/us/david-dorn-st-louis-police-shot-trnd/index.html.

14. "Murphy Supports Peaceful Protests, Distinguishes Between Nail Salons and Justice for Murder," Insider NJ, June 1, 2020, https://www.insidernj.com/murphy-supports-peaceful-protests-new-jersey-can-leader/.

15. America's Founding Documents, "Declaration of Independence: A Transcription," National Archives, accessed November 19, 2019, https://www.archives.gov/founding-docs/declaration-transcript.

16. Brad Devereaux, "Moviegoers Pack Michigan Drive-In Theater, Defying Whitmer's Stay-Home Order," M Live, updated May 16, 2020, https://www.mlive.com/coronavirus/2020/05/moviegoers-wait-in-long-lines-to-get-into-michigan-drive-in-that-opened-despite-stay-at-home-order.html.

17. Patrick McGreevy, "California Pot Dispensaries Are Open during Coronavirus Crisis. Some Want Them Closed," *Los Angeles Times*, March 30, 2020, https://www.latimes.com/california/story/2020-03-30/california-cannabis-dispensaries-essential-businesses-coronavirus-crisis; KTVU staff, "The Complete List of California's Essential Workers," KTVU FOX 2, March 25, 2020, https://www.ktvu.com/news/the-complete-list-of-californias-essential-workers.

18. Zack Smith, "Despite Win in Wisconsin, Religious Discrimination Remains During Lockdown," The Heritage Foundation, June 10, 2020, https://www.heritage.org/religious-liberty/commentary/despite-win-wisconsin-religious-discrimination-remains-during-lockdown.

19. Evelyn Beatrice Hall, *The Friends of Voltaire* (New York: G. P. Putnam's Sons, 1907), 199.

20. Tom Cotton, "Tom Cotton: Send In the Troops," *New York Times*, June 3, 2020, https://www.nytimes.com/2020/06/03/opinion/tom-cotton-protests-military.html.

21. Elahe Izadi, Paul Farhi, and Sarah Ellison, "After Staff Uproar, New York Times Says Sen. Tom Cotton Op-Ed Urging Military Incursion into U.S. Cities 'Did Not Meet Our Standards,'" *Washington Post*, June 4, 2020, https://www.washingtonpost.com/media/2020/06/03/new-york-times-tom-cotton/.

22. Matt Taibbi, "The American Press Is Destroying Itself," Reporting by Matt Taibbi, June 12, 2020, https://taibbi.substack.com/p/the-news-media-is-destroying-itself.

23. Max Cohen, "New York Times Opinion Writer Bari Weiss Resigns, Citing Hostile Culture and Lack of Ideological Diversity," Politico.com, July 14, 2020, https://www.politico.com/news/2020/07/14/new-york-times-bari-weiss-resigns-360730.

24. Scott Hennen, *Grass Roots: A Commonsense Action Agenda for America* (New York: Simon & Schuster, 2011), 234.

25. Jennifer Schuessler and Elizabeth A. Harris, "Artists and Writers Warn of an 'Intolerant Climate.' Reaction Is Swift," *New York Times*, July 7, 2020, https://www.nytimes.com/2020/07/07/arts/harpers-letter.html.

26. Tim Hains, "Spotlight: Seattle CBS Affiliate Films Looter Leaving Cheesecake Factory Carrying an Entire Cheesecake," RealClearPolitics, May 31, 2020, https://www.realclearpolitics.com/video/2020/05/31/spotlight_seattle_cbs_affailiate_films_looter_leaving_cheesecake_factory_carrying_an_entire_cheesecake.html; news anchor dialogue transcribed from embedded video.

27. Taibbi, "The American Press Is Destroying Itself."

28. Kyle Smith, "This Is Easy: Don't Excuse, Defend, or Encourage Rioters," *National Review*, May 29, 2020, https://www.nationalreview.com/2020/05/this-is-easy-dont-excuse-defend-or-encourage-rioters/.

29. Smith, "This Is Easy."

30. Rob Tornoe, "Photos of Defaced Statue of Philly Abolitionist Matthias Baldwin Go Viral," *Philadelphia Inquirer*, June 12, 2020, https://www.inquirer.com/news/philadelphia-protests-matthias-baldwin-statue-abolitionist-twitter-photos-20200612.html.
31. Ruby Gonzales, "Statue of Abolitionist John Greenleaf Whittier Vandalized in His Namesake City," WDN, June 15, 2020, https://www.whittierdailynews.com/2020/06/15/statue-of-abolitionist-john-greenleaf-whittier-vandalized-in-his-namesake-city/.
32. Ryan McMaken, " 'Protesters' Deface Bust of Miguel Cervantes, a Former Slave," Mises Institute, June 22, 2020, https://mises.org/wire/protestors-deface-bust-miguel-cervantes-former-slave.
33. Eliott C. McLaughlin, "Honoring the Unforgivable: The Horrific Acts Behind the Names on America's Infamous Monuments and Tributes," CNN, June 17, 2020, https://www.cnn.com/2020/06/16/us/racist-statues-controversial-monuments-in-america-robert-lee-columbus/index.html.
34. Deroy Murdock, "Looting and Rioting After George Floyd Killing Draw Shocking Support From Left" Fox News, June 9, 2020, https://www.foxnews.com/opinion/george-floyd-democrats-police-deroy-murdock.

Chapter 6

1. Robby Soave, "The 1793 Project Unmasked," *Reason*, June 12, 2020, https://reason.com/2020/06/12/protesters-activists-shor-floyd-1793-project/.
2. "Bamiyan Buddhas," *National Geographic*, accessed October 26, 2020, https://www.nationalgeographic.org/photo/bamiyan-buddahs/; "Bamiyan," Britannica, accessed October 26, 2020, https://www.britannica.com/place/Bamiyan.
3. "The Notre-Dame Cathedral Was Nearly Destroyed By French Revolutionary Mobs," History, accessed October 26, 2020, https://www.history.com/news/notre-dame-fire-french-revolution.

4. Howard Zinn, *A People's History of the United States: 1492–Present*, 3rd ed. (New York: Routledge, 2013), 9–10.
5. John Adams, "Argument for the Defense," December 3–4, 1770, Founders Online, https://founders.archives. gov/documents/Adams/05-03-02-0001-0004-0016.
6. "An Experts' History of Howard Zinn," *Los Angeles Times*, February 1, 2010, https://www.latimes.com/ archives/la-xpm-2010-feb-01-la-oe-miller1-2010feb01-story.html.
7. Mary Grabar, *Debunking Howard Zinn: Exposing the Fake History That Turned a Generation Against America* (Washington, DC: Regnery, 2019), front matter.
8. Mary Grabar, "AHI's Mary Grabar: Why I Wrote Debunking Howard Zinn," Alexander Hamilton Institute, August 20, 2019, https://www.theahi.org/ahis-mary-grabar-why-i-wrote-debunking-howard-zinn/.
9. Mary Grabar, "How Howard Zinn Helped Propel Efforts to Erase Columbus Day," *The Federalist*, October 14, 2019, https://thefederalist.com/2019/10/14/how-howard-zinn-helped-propel-efforts-to-erase-columbus-day/.
10. Abraham Lincoln, "Lincoln on America," National Park Service, accessed July 29, 2020, https://www.nps.gov/ liho/learn/historyculture/onamerica.htm.
11. Abraham Lincoln, "The Gettysburg Address," Abraham Lincoln Online, accessed July 29, 2020, http://www. abrahamlincolnonline.org/lincoln/speeches/gettysburg. htm.
12. James Lindsay, "Saying No to Critical Race Theory," New Discourses podcast, July 20, 2020, https:// newdiscourses.com/2020/07/saying-no-critical-race-theory/.
13. James Lindsay, "2+2 Never Equals 5," New Discourses, August 3, 2020, https://newdiscourses.com/2020/08/2-plus-2-never-equals-5/.
14. Sophia Ankel, "Black Lives Matter Protesters Caught on Video Smashing up a Restaurant and Ordering Diners to Leave As Unrest Continues in Rochester for Fourth Night," Insider.com, September 6, 2020, https://www.insider.com/

watch-rochester-blm-protesters-intimidate-diners-to-leave-restaurant-2020-9; Charles Davis, "A Viral Video of White Protesters Yelling at a Restaurant Patron to Support Black Lives Matter Is Being Ridiculed by Pretty Much Everyone," BusinessInsider.com, August 25, 2020, https://www.businessinsider.com/white-protesters-confront-diners-during-black-lives-matter-protest-2020-8.

15. Lee Fang (@lhfang), "Asked everyone I spoke with today if there was anything they wanted to get off their chest about the movement," Twitter, June 3, 2020, 11:54 p.m., https://twitter.com/lhfang/status/1268390704645943297.

16. Akela Lacy (@akela_lacy), "Tired of being made to deal with my coworker @lhfang continuing to push narratives about black on black on black crime after repeatedly being asked not to," Twitter, June 4, 2020, 12:06 a.m., https://twitter.com/akela_lacy/status/1268393571121496066.

17. Akela Lacy, June 4, 2020, comment on Twitter, "Tired of being made to deal with my coworker."

18. Taibbi, "The American Press Is Destroying Itself."

19. "What We Believe," Black Lives Matter, accessed August 10, 2020, https://blacklivesmatter.com/what-we-believe/.

20. Jared Ball, "A Short History of Black Lives Matter," July 22, 2015, YouTube video, 7:10, https://www.youtube.com/watch?time_continue=448&v=kCghDx5qN4s&feature=emb_logo.

21. John 8:31–32, 36.

22. Abraham Lincoln, "Lyceum Address," Abraham Lincoln Online, accessed July 29, 2020, http://www.abrahamlincolnonline.org/lincoln/speeches/lyceum.htm.

Chapter 7

1. Shaun King (@shaunking), "Yes, I think the statues of the white European they claim is Jesus should also come down.... Tear them down." Twitter, June 22, 2020, 12:42 p.m., https://twitter.com/shaunking/status/127510 6946916499456?lang=en.

2. John Oxenham, "In Christ There Is No East or West" (1908, public domain), https://hymnary.org/text/in_christ_there_is_no_east_or_west_oxenh.
3. Jordan Davidson, "As They Turn To Burning Bibles, Portland Rioters Show Their True Colors," *The Federalist*, August 1, 2020, https://thefederalist.com/2020/08/01/as-they-turn-to-burning-bibles-portland-rioters-show-their-true-colors/.
4. Luke 23:34, KJV.
5. Sam Harris, "Can We Pull Back From the Brink?," Making Sense Podcast transcript, June 18, 2020, https://samharris.org/can-pull-back-brink/.
6. Krista West, *The Basics of Metals and Metalloids* (New York: Rosen Publishing Group, 2014), 81.
7. Kate Shellnutt, "What Is Billy Graham's Friendship With Martin Luther King Jr. Worth?," *Christianity Today*, February 23, 2018, https://www.christianitytoday.com/news/2018/february/billy-graham-martin-luther-king-jr-friendship-civil-rights.html.
8. Caleb Parke, "Blind Woman Banned From Park for Two Years for Sharing Jesus," Fox News, June 17, 2020, https://www.foxnews.com/us/christian-woman-rhode-island-park-discrimination-lawsuit.

Epilogue

1. Clifton Fadiman and André Bernard, eds., *Bartlett's Book of Anecdotes* (New York: Little, Brown and Company, 2000), 211.
2. "Powerless at Pearl Harbor: USS *New Orleans*," Pearl Harbor Visitors Bureau, accessed October 26, 2020, https://visitpearlharbor.org/powerless-at-pearl-harbor-uss-new-orleans/.
3. Chuck Colson, "Thirty Pints of Blood," *Christian Post*, March 8, 2007, https://www.christianpost.com/news/thirty-pints-of-blood.html.

Connect with
Dr. Michael Youssef!

Follow Dr. Youssef for life-giving truth, behind-the-scenes ministry updates, and much more.

MichaelYoussef.com

 MichaelAYoussef

Michael A. Youssef

Discover More

from Michael Youssef and
Leading The Way